Happy 42nd
Anniversary!
♡, Linda

& Many
More to come!.

My Italian Garden

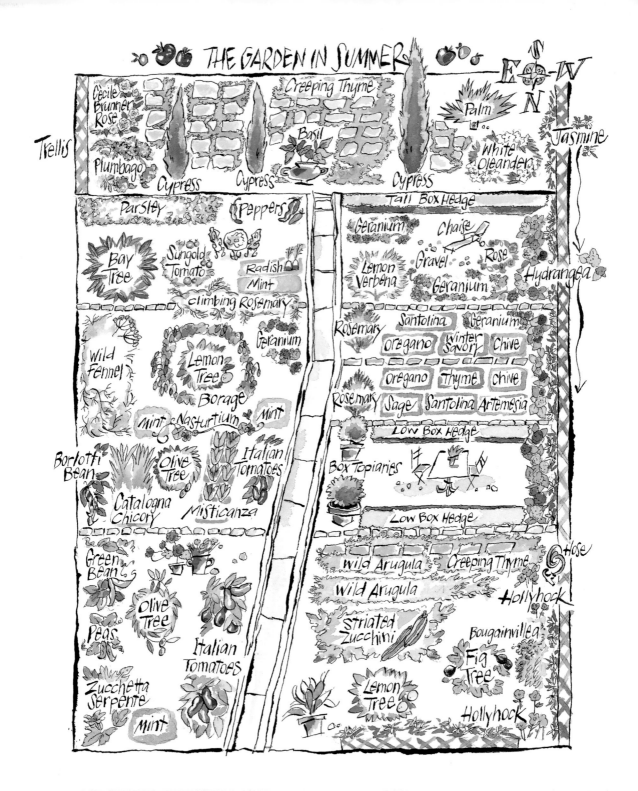

My Italian Garden

Viana La Place

Illustrations by Cindy Salans Rosenheim

BROADWAY BOOKS   NEW YORK

PUBLISHED BY BROADWAY BOOKS

Published in the United States by Broadway Books,
an imprint of The Doubleday Broadway Publishing Group,
a division of Random House, Inc., New York.
www.broadwaybooks.com

BROADWAY BOOKS and its logo, a letter B bisected on the diagonal,
are trademarks of Random House, Inc.

Book design by Elizabeth Rendfleisch

Library of Congress Cataloging-in-Publication Data
La Place, Viana.
My Italian garden : more than 125 seasonal recipes from a garden inspired by
Italy / by Viana La Place. —1st ed.
p. cm.
Includes bibliographical references and index.
(alk. paper) 1. Cookery, Italian. 2. Kitchen gardens. I. Title.

TX723.L255 2007
641.5'945—dc22
2006030248

ISBN: 978-0-7679-1825-1

PRINTED IN JAPAN

1 3 5 7 9 10 8 6 4 2

First Edition

To Pino
con tenerezza

CONTENTS

ACKNOWLEDGMENTS

I would like to thank the following people for their contributions, encouragement, and kindness: Jennifer Josephy, my editor; Fred Hill, my literary agent; Nina Thompson, for invaluable assistance; and Wendy Downing, who helped test recipes.

And a special expression of thanks to my illustrator, Cindy Salans Rosenheim, for so sensitively evoking the spirit of my Italian garden.

My Italian Garden

• Introduction •

MY IMAGE OF AN ITALIAN GARDEN was formed long before I actually saw one. It began with stories my mother told me of the veranda that wrapped around the apartment in the palazzo her grandmother owned, where my mother grew up. The wide balcony on the second floor of the building was filled with a profusion of plants—succulents, geraniums, jasmine.

The other garden brought to life by my mother's descriptions was at Villino Riccardo, situated in the foothills of Monte Pellegrino, the famous mountain of Palermo. This was their home when Palermo's city heat became too hot to endure. In those days this area was all villas and countryside. The garden produced fruits and flowers, vegetables and herbs. A huge fig tree was located just behind the tall iron gates leading into the villa. Parsley, basil, and mint, the basis for so many southern Italian dishes, formed one section of the garden. Tomatoes, some for salads, others for sauce, grew in profusion. A special zucchini, long, thin, and pale green, grown on a pergola, dangled by the hundreds among large, shady leaves. A sparkling little fountain created a cooling effect even when the gravel crunching beneath one's footsteps radiated heat. Roses were so fragrant and lush in the humid heat of summer my mother felt she might faint from the overpoweringly sweet perfume emanating from the fleshy petals.

The very first garden in my own life was part of my family's first home in America, in California's San Gabriel Valley. I spent my infancy and early childhood there. Persimmon trees, peach trees, and wild berries grew in this garden. When I arrived on the scene, I instinctively loved being in this untamed leafy paradise and soon acquired the nickname La Piccola Contadina, the little country girl, as well as the aristocratic sobriquet La Baronessa, the Baroness. To this day, they remain the two sides of my personality!

It wasn't until I was twelve years old that we finally traveled to Italy. After visiting relatives in Rome, with its exotic, yet strangely familiar sights and smells, we journeyed by train to Sicily. My face pressed against the train window, I took in all the sights, some familiar, others unusual and captivating—palms, oleanders, rough rocks, gnarled olive trees, and then the stunning blue of the Mediterranean.

In Palermo, in Taormina, in Agrigento—wherever we traveled, I fell deeply and completely in love with the rugged landscape. Wild fennel grew tall on cliffs by the sea. *Nespole,* or loquat trees, with wide, corrugated dark green leaves, provided some welcome shade. The fruit's mottled skin, the color of apricots, contained perfumed flesh and two large chestnut-colored seeds. There were dusty dwarf date palms with sprays of dark gold fruits and tall bushy oleanders, heavily flowered with floppy, powder-sweet-scented petals in Tunisian red, peach, and creamy white.

In Bonpietro, my father's town, behind the country home of relatives was a large walled garden, beyond which stretched miles of countryside. I stood on the upstairs balcony looking out on the garden. Apricots, their complexions lightly speckled and ruddy; golden plums, the smallest I'd ever seen; and peaches, flushed red, were tantalizing delights. The zucchini hidden among tangles of large green leaves startled me with saffron blossoms open wide in the sun. Down in the garden, I bent over to smell heavily spiced carnations, picked an apricot and felt its warmth in my hand, bit into its fleshy sweetness.

After graduating from college, I returned to Italy to begin my own explorations. I would arrive in Rome and head south to the Amalfi coast, Sicily, and smaller islands—Ustica, off the coast of Palermo; Capri, a short boat ride from Naples; and numerous isolated dots in the sea. But in search of the Italy described to me by my parents, the Italy I had in my imagination, I headed off the beaten path to Puglia, all the way to the Basso Salento. This southernmost part of the province of Lecce is located at the very end of the heel of boot-shaped Italy. I knew it would be primarily agricultural, a land of olive groves and sea.

Arriving, I immediately felt at home. I knew it was a place I would return to again and again. Traditional Italian culture made me feel as though I had traveled back in time. Since most people I encountered spoke only Italian, and tourists were practically nonexistent, I felt I had found the real Italy.

The Salento has many natural gifts. The pristine sea changes from palest aquamarine to sapphire at the horizon line. The mineral-rich red clay soil produces extraordinary cultivated fruits and vegetables as well as potent, aromatic wild herbs and greens. But it is primarily a land of olive trees stretching as far as the eye can see, until suddenly one catches a glimpse of the glinting, brilliant Mediterranean. The landscape colors are muted shades of green, pewter, and silver. Limestone rocks look as though a giant hand had randomly strewn them about. The same golden-hued limestone is seen in the drystone walls that divide parcels of land or wind sinuously through the countryside to delineate narrow roads.

I found a human-scale existence and a deeply rooted sense of community. Being a stranger in town, I was overwhelmed by the generosity extended to me. The soulful people gave me a sense of belonging. The wild countryside, the agriculture, community, the local cooking—all touched me profoundly.

I created my current Italian garden based on the six summers I spent in a small town by the sea in the Salento. Each summer I returned to the same two-story villa, renting the top floor from a bright and lively ninety-year-old retired schoolteacher. A large balcony overlooked the constantly changing sea. In back, off the big bedroom, another terrace faced other villas, pine trees, bougainvilleas, and oleanders.

During these long periods, I lived the life of an Italian. New friends cooked for me and patiently answered questions. I found gifts on my doorstep—local breads and biscotti for me to sample. Pino Plantera, a kindred spirit, became a close friend and guide. He shared his knowledge of wild plants, botany, geology, archaeology, and more, taking me to places I would never have discovered on my own. His education is as an agronomist, but his passion lies in the olive groves he owns. He began to tend them organically long before organics were in the news, learning how to do so by unearthing old manuscripts long buried in archives, which he dusted off, studied, and implemented.

Under Pino's watchful eye, I worked in his olive groves. He took me on excursions to the countryside and seaside to teach me about all the amazing and diverse wild plants. We picked wild arugula and pulled up bulbs of wild garlic. I smelled the sweet perfume of wild mint and earthy savory under my feet as I walked behind him, attempting to keep up with his boundless energy. The commingled perfumes of salty sea breezes, wild herbs, burning olive wood, and warm pine were a balm and a tonic, heightening my senses.

It is the plants, flowers, and wild herbs of the Salento and Sicily that I grow in my Italian garden in San Francisco. My *giardino Italiano* transports me to the Italy I love. All I have to do is open my kitchen door to feel its embrace.

Creating My Italian Garden

What was once a very long shady stretch of sloping land was transformed in three days into a sunlit virgin canvas for the creation of my Italian garden. Two fir trees planted by a child seventy years ago had been topped off too often so as not to obstruct the view of the bay. This had created trees with dangerously long and heavy branches.

One day, four men with chain saws arrived. With pulleys and ropes holding them safely attached to the trunks, they climbed the enormous trees and, bit by bit, the firs disappeared. Out of a dim forest where forlorn vinca, ferns, and baby tears had ruled—an unwelcoming place, impossible to cultivate—a sunlit garden space emerged. I marveled at the dramatic change from darkness to light. Now I could create a real garden and I knew what I wanted.

Like a woman possessed, I shoveled the soil to create six level terraces, three on each side of an old cement walkway, and at the back, up a few steps, a long terrace running the full width of the garden. Seven terraces in all.

In the course of digging, I found, among other treasures, a huge stockpile of gravel from a long-ago renovation, which I incorporated into the terraces. It was a relentless, monthlong struggle to level all the terraces. While working, I planned. Some terraces would become living areas; others would be left fallow for planting.

A windfall came my way when I was able to salvage a truckload of broken sidewalk concrete, an aggregate composed of stones and cement. The truck was just about to take off for the city dump. For sixty dollars, they brought it all to the front of my home, unloaded it, and drove away. Those oddly shaped pieces were just what I needed.

As each terrace was leveled, drystone walls had to be put in place to hold back the earth for the next terrace. I used the broken chunks to create low walls. Wicky, a college student I met who was working for a landscaper across the street, assisted me in laying the stones. No mortar was used in this painstaking, time-honored craft. You simply strategize which stones will connect into secure and snug-fitting positions. Drystone walls are the very soul of the Italian garden; therefore nothing else would do. As the work progressed, I was amazed and gratified that salvaged sidewalk ended up looking like stone walls that had been in place for hundreds of years.

At the end of this period of intense labor, I began with foundation plants and started the herb garden. I ponder this still-new Italian garden of mine first thing every morning, standing where two large windows meet in the corner of the kitchen. Sometimes it is still dark outside and I can barely make out the outlines of the plants. When the garden is sunlit, the golden morning light reveals all the vibrant color and shades of green. I stand here doing all my garden dreaming. How I wish the slow-growing palm tree I recently planted were twenty-five feet tall instead of a mere six-foot specimen.

The cypress trees are tall, elegant spires that define the depth of the landscape. I watch them carefully since they need excellent drainage and can easily become diseased. Here in San Francisco's moist, cool climate, cypress trees do grow but must be protected from too much water and wind. What self-respecting garden could call itself Italian without at least one cypress? I have three and cherish each one.

I sculpted a rangy, European bay tree into a towering, plump column, risking my life in the process. Standing at the top of a very tall ladder to get to the uppermost branches, I hung on to the tree with one hand to maintain my balance and sawed with the other.

San Francisco's neighborhoods are a series of different microclimates. Some are quite warm, others hidden in fog. I am lucky since my garden is in a sun-pocket, even though it is on the northern side of the city near the Golden Gate Bridge. The garden is blessed with tall retaining walls of concrete. Over the years they have taken on the patina of an old Italian villa. I used techniques to generate greater warmth for my Italian landscape. I brought in more gravel and boulders, fragments of broken terra-cotta pots, and large stones.

These elements merge with tomatoes, greens, fruit trees, and aromatic shrubs and flowers. When I sit in the garden on a hot day, heat rising up from the gravel, sur-rounded by my plants, I feel I am close to Italy, even though it is thousands of miles away.

The Philosophy That Guides My Garden and This Book

The challenge I set for myself in writing this book was to feature as the basic ingredi-ent in recipes only what my garden can grow. To this, I've added gifts from fellow gar-deners and neighbors, staying true to the communal spirit I've experienced so often in Italy.

When eating garden produce, the concept of seasonal cooking becomes a reality. You pick just what is needed for the meal you are about to prepare. This allows you to taste the vegetables, herbs, and fruits in a direct and powerful way. An artichoke cut from the stalk and brought straight into the kitchen and sautéed in a bit of olive oil will make you feel you are tasting an artichoke for the first time. Its rich mineral taste and tender texture are a revelation. Pinching off a sprig of basil warmed by the sun brings a rush of sensory pleasure—one sprig is all you need to flavor a tomato sauce since the essential oils are all vibrantly present. Plucking a ripe lemon sends a dreamy wave of citrus perfume into the air. Lemons lose essential oils quickly; within thirty minutes they begin to dissipate. The lemon you carry to the kitchen to squeeze on a freshly cooked plate of greens will be wildly fragrant. Salad greens cut for lunch and then again for dinner will be incredibly crisp or tender, depending on the variety.

The same attributes that mean better taste and texture are also pleasurable signs that you are receiving maximum nutritive value. The less time that passes from harvesting produce to placing it on your dinner plate means greater and more complete nourishment.

Cooking from the garden is uncomplicated cooking. Why add extraneous ingredients to flavorful produce? In fact, you will want to keep preparations pure and simple to enjoy what you've harvested in its pristine state.

All the recipes in this book reflect the themes of seasonality, simplicity, and freshness. This is garden-style cooking, and it makes being in the kitchen a joy rather than a chore. Time spent preparing dishes is minimal and the rewards are great.

Each day as I wander through my garden I am amazed by changes, large and small. Is it possible the figs are plumping up so quickly? Bordering one of the lemon trees, tall stalks of borage have shot up, bearing clusters of starry blue blossoms that form a magical ring around the tree. I check for zucchini to pick. They should never be longer than four or five inches, so I keep a watchful eye. I almost instinctively bend to cut the arugula leaves that grow in profusion to add to a salad or pasta sauce.

When I enter the kitchen, my basket brimming with chicory, tomatoes, a lemon, and sprigs of herbs, it is the garden that has guided me in what dishes I will prepare. Peering into the basket, I'm overwhelmed by nature's extravagant beauty and aromas. I can already taste the juices of scarlet red tomatoes I will cut into wedges for a salad.

An Italian garden is really a state of mind. You do not need an elaborate villa to create your Italian garden. The essence of Italy can be captured in pots on a sunny terrace or a shaded balcony. An Italian garden can be herbs growing on a sunny windowsill or the back steps. You can grow your garden on a large parcel of land or on a tiny patch of earth. I hope you will be inspired by my Italian garden to grow one of your own, no matter what the size, and experience the joys of cooking directly from your Italian garden.

SUMMER

SUMMER IN SAN FRANCISCO is usually a dismal affair—cold, foggy, and rainy. Across the Golden Gate Bridge, the wine country taunts me with its truly Mediterranean climate. There, I know I could grow anything my heart desires.

But some special saint or angel must have had a part in this first summer of cultivating my Italian garden. San Francisco is experiencing a steady stream of sun and heat. Not the profound heat and humidity that is the Mediterranean, but real warmth from a plentitude of sunshine.

This is a good summer to be growing a garden of tomatoes, zucchini, and figs. My climate is always perfect for greens such as chicories and lettuces, for artichokes and tart citrus, but summer fruits and vegetables are a challenge.

After much planning, dreaming, and fantasizing, the reality of growing the summer garden sets in. Hard work, lots of it, keeps the garden in good form. My neighbor Giovanni's figs come early in the season. They are luscious as warm honey. This Adriatic fig's color is startling under the thin, light green skin—violet-pink flesh, surrounded by a sweet, white protective blanket. Plump and juicy, each one is a voluptuous indulgence, especially when just picked. Giovanni washes the figs lightly in his garden's old water basin with his wrinkled, knowing hands. Fruits warm from the sun expand and amplify in flavor and fragrance. Even my sometimes moody occasional assistant Wicky is speechless with delight when he tastes the figs Giovanni shares with us over the fence.

I've watched Giovanni and his wife Ginetta for years, and learned from them. Almost every day they descend their stairs and make the rounds of the garden. Giovanni has a long-handled tool for weeding, since it's getting harder for him to bend down without feeling breathless. I see Ginetta every morning, her housecoat under a functional raincoat, umbrella in hand on rainy days. In summer or warm weather, she simply wears a housecoat and a baseball cap to shield her eyes.

They appear first thing in the morning, rain or shine. I observe them at least two other crucial times during the day, just before lunch and just before dinner. That's when they harvest what will be incorporated into that day's meal. I'm often jealous. What will Ginetta cook today? I love Ginetta's cooking. Her vegetable soup, made entirely from their garden, is one I would gladly consume daily.

Wicky got a chance to sample the soup when she prepared lunch for us after Wicky had finished helping in their garden. Their generosity, again so much a part of the communal Italian spirit, is always immensely gladdening. "More soup? More bread?" asks Ginetta. To Wicky, Giovanni says, "How about some scrambled eggs and bacon?" I translate the Italian, since they speak English with hesitation. "How about some Campari?" asks Giovanni. "Sure," says Wicky. "Thanks. Grazie." He likes to learn and would enjoy speaking to them in Italian.

Wicky, six feet three inches tall with dreamy brown eyes, an accomplished competitive rower and mountain climber, comes equipped with an overactive intellect. Giovanni plants by the moon. Wicky wants to understand scientifically why. He and I ponder it and theories arise. My feeling is that it's been done for centuries, so why question the wisdom of agricultural history?

Giovanni and Ginetta's is a working garden. No place to sit, no terra-cotta-colored umbrella with table and chairs, no chaise lounges, no statuary or fancy pots with embellishments. Occasionally, on a really hot day, Giovanni will pull out an old folding chair, the kind with striped mesh ribbons, and sit in the shade of a tree to drink a beer. I've never seen Ginetta sit in the garden. She's too busy. It's a working garden all right, and Ginetta has little patience for tricky flowers and elaborate Tuscan urns, even though both Ginetta and her husband are Tuscan, from Lucca.

They relate to the earth in a way that is in tune with nature. Ginetta does, in fact, cultivate the most glorious cymbidium orchids on the large terrace above the roomy shed that overlooks their very long, narrow garden. A geranium grows near the shed, a few gladioli, and a single rosebush. Recently, I noticed some climbing sweet peas on Ginetta's garden wall. I have a hunch these were planted for her little granddaughter, who has grown up in the garden.

Ginetta certainly doesn't have time for a rose garden, and I don't blame her. I've discovered that only certain roses grow well here, especially the rugosa variety. All others, no matter how vigilant one is, will have black spots, rust, and mildew unless sprayed with chemicals, not a part of my organic garden.

Ginetta and Giovanni have watched my garden grow and change with great curiosity and encouragement. They've even asked if they could possibly have a few of the seeds I use, and they take only a few. I want to give them packetsful for all their friendship, their sharing of life stories, sad times, and happy times over the garden fence.

In my own garden, a stranger to tomato growing would be aghast. The leaves are dry, brown, and brittle, seemingly scandalously left to wither and die. But this is the secret to growing good tomatoes. Once the fruits have begun to form, hold off on water. Don't give in to a natural tendency to keep growth green and resplendent. Pino, my friend in Puglia, said, when I watched him water his little local tomatoes, "The tomatoes need just an eyedropperful of water. Water sparingly for the best taste."

Tomatoes are turning out to be the glory of my summer Italian garden and a great surprise. Large Costoluto tomatoes have incredibly steep ridges—amazing in shape, each one with particular and peculiar contours, each exhibiting uniquely high shoulders and deep indentations.

Principe Borghese tomatoes grow well and in abundance. They are good in salads and sauces. I use them often and always have a basketful on the kitchen counter ready for salads, soups, and pastas.

I planted the San Marzano tomatoes with a reckless feeling of "Why not try?" They are native to San Marzano, a town in the hot, hot Campagna region. To my surprise, the fruits form beautifully in their distinctive oval and elongated shape, turn from lime green, to pale pink, to crimson. As good as they look, and as prolific the fruiting, the real story always takes place during the harvest. Mealy flesh and not much flavor leave me feeling crestfallen.

To counter my disappointment, I start harvesting them while still greenish, barely streaked with red. Rather than the full-flavored sauce-making tomatoes they are meant to be, I use them as crisp and tart additions to salads, risottos, and panini. Adaptability in the garden is another good trait to develop.

To be honest, the most successful tomato in the garden is a miniature variety, the Sungold cherry tomato. The seedling was given to me by a gardening friend, and it produces and produces. The fruits are sweet and the flesh firm. Not Italian and not even rare, the Sungold is a sure-fire source for summer salads, soups, and pastas. The tomatoes trail up and around the bamboo teepee I erected. The structure looks like a Christmas tree with little glowing golden balls that seem almost capable of illuminating the garden at night.

I had to place an emergency phone call to Wicky (who appears when he can, depending on his school schedule) when the tomato cages we used began tipping and falling from the weight of the fruit. We attempted to prop up particularly heavy branches using bamboo poles as crutches.

Then tragedy struck one day. I was attempting to lift off the ground a particularly heavily laden branch of Costoluto tomatoes, perhaps ten in all, and raise it onto a support, when it simply snapped at the stem into my hands.

I was unable to part with it. Rather than simply abandon it to the heap of garden debris, I carried it with solemn ceremony to the kitchen, amazed at the weight of the broken branch of green tomatoes. It felt like a dead body carried to its final resting place—my kitchen counter. For days I looked at the branch with a heavy heart, upset at my lack of forethought. Secretly, though, and with a sneaky sense of guilt, I thought the branch was sublimely beautiful. The unripe fruits in shades of green, from palest lime to emerald, were surrounded with crinkly brown leaves that turned to dust when I touched one. The dry, gnarled tomato stem was strangely captivating—a twisted, sculptural form. It remained in my kitchen for a long time, the tomatoes turning an odd greenish-pink color but remaining preternaturally firm.

Nasturtiums grow almost too prolifically, out of control. They arrive unannounced and proceed to pop up everywhere. The tender, peppery nasturtium leaves go into chopped salads. The petals adorn sweet and savory dishes. I pick the buds to cure in sea salt as a substitute for capers. I could not muster the courage even to attempt to grow that enchanting Mediterranean plant, the caper. Its fragrant blossoms and rounded leaves grow between the stones of fortresses in trailing cascades, scenting hot, humid Italian nights. I thought it didn't have a chance, at least not in my San Francisco microclimate.

Those nasturtiums wind their way up and around any and all possible supports. String bean poles and tomato teepees aren't immune. Climbing borlotti beans and peas are entwined with their blossoms. The leaves are a magnet for snails hiding in the shade of the largest saucer-shaped leaves. With the lovely blossom comes the risk of snail attacks, so I am always on the lookout.

The rose geranium grows and grows and blossoms profusely. It begins to sicken me slightly as summer progresses. Its odd roselike smell is musty and pungent, not soft and sweet. I keep hacking it back, pruning it into ever smaller attractive shapes. One day, I keep pruning until nothing is left. I feel greatly relieved. I no longer have to worry about brushing against it while working in the herb garden and releasing a huge wave of its scent.

In its place I plant an artemisia that grows like silver lace, smells of fresh sea air, and glistens magically when watered. It's a fast grower. It shoots up to nearly five feet tall rather quickly. I keep it beautifully pruned in a graceful rounded shape.

I decide to do a deeper pruning of the artemisia. I'm shocked to find that the soft exterior foliage conceals an inner torment of dead leaves, a contorted confusion of thick, rough stems, completely devoid of the downy leaves I so love to touch. I learn. Now I'll hard-prune the artemisia to keep it leafy inside and out.

I am a cruel master of herbs. No water, ever. But I know they love my mean neglect, especially in this mild climate of mine. The aromatic oils become distilled potent flavor and scent. Only the tender herbs, basil and parsley, must be watered or the leaves will be droopy, not crisp and succulent.

When I planted the fig tree I couldn't contain my joy. It was a small but sturdy tree. Now I watch and wait. The fuzzy fig leaves grow bigger and bigger. The fruits first appear tiny as beads, then swell and plump to large teardrop shapes, transforming from green to deepest eggplant when ripe. The San Piero variety, here called rather prosaically the Brown Turkey fig, matures in late summer. My thought was the figs could fully ripen in the greatest heat that usually comes at the end of summer and into fall.

The resulting figs are flavorful but not very juicy. They are certainly not as good as Giovanni's figs. Still, each of my San Piero figs is more precious to me than the Crown jewels, or the Hope diamond. I pick each one carefully and place it in my small basket. I would like more fig trees, an orchard's worth.

Here is an important lesson in planting: Remember, no matter how small the seedling, plants grow bigger! Make sure to find out how much space is needed when they grow to full maturity. I learned this when planting zucchini. All varieties require an enormous amount of space.

The zucchini plants in my garden ramble and sprawl. The leaves grow bigger and bigger and bigger. Tender stems turn to thick, fibrous stalks. One plant produces an enormous amount of zucchini and saffron, non-fruit-bearing male blossoms, also delicate and delicious to eat. Actually, the entire plant is edible—tender leaves, vegetables, and flowers, each with its own distinctive taste and texture.

I planted a cucumber variety that I remember with pleasure eating together with Pino, my friend and guide, in his olive grove in the Salento. The young plants were victims of snails when I attempted to grow them in my garden. I am not sure they would have ripened to full sweetness, hinting of melon, since intense heat is required.

It is a delight to go into the summer garden early in the morning. I search between the tumble of zucchini leaves to find brilliantly sunlit blossoms opening petals to the sun. I fill my garden basket with zucchini and blossoms for today's enjoyment at the kitchen table.

Along the way, I meander around the terraced beds to gather a few herbs and pick one or two borage flowers to nibble on, always amazed at their hint of cucumber flavor. I stroke the lush artemisia bush, bury my face in its velvety perfumed leaves, and inhale deeply.

Surveying my summer Italian garden, I am pleased that so much has grown vigorously and well. The tomato leaves look dead as can be but through experience I know better. I look at the tomatoes and think of Pino in his Pugliese garden, of all I have learned and have yet to learn.

ANTIPASTI · *Starters*

Fresh Ricotta with Basil and Parsley 19

La Baronessa's Roses 20

Tiny Herb Frittatas 22

Ricotta and Caprino Layered with Fresh Basil Leaves 24

Hard-cooked Eggs Wrapped in Giant Basil Leaves 26

INSALATE · *Salads*

Meyer Lemon and Cucumber Salad with Mint 28

Zucchini Carpaccio with Almonds 29

Summer Caprese 30

Parsley and Rice Salad 32

Avocado on the Half-Shell 34

MINESTRE · *Soups*

Soup with New Potatoes, Saffron, Basil, and Mascarpone 35

Barley Soup with Summer Herbs 36

PASTA

Spaghettini with Basil Leaves and Strands of Lemon Zest 37

Spaghetti with Tomato Sauce and Fresh Basil Leaves 38

Orecchiette with Little Yellow Tomatoes and Parsley 39

Tubetti La Favorita 40

Pasta with Almost Every Herb in the Garden 41

RISOTTO

Risotto with Zucchino Striato d'Italia 43

Risotto Verde 44

PIATTI FORTI · *Main Dishes*

Bread "Lasagna"   45

Potato, Olive, and Ricotta Torta   47

Rolled Thin Frittata Filled with Ricotta and Parsley   49

Frittata Fiorita   51

VERDURE · *Vegetables*

Green Beans with European-style Butter and Basil Leaves   52

Little Golden Tomatoes Sautéed with Green and Black Olives and Parsley   53

Sicilian Zucchini al Picchi Pacchi   54

Mushrooms and Bread Slices on Rosemary Branch Skewers   55

PIZZA AND PANINI

Pino's Pizza   57

Garden Herb Pizza with Parma Prosciutto Topping   60

Panini with Grilled Zucchini, Ricotta Salata, and Basil   62

CONDIMENTI · *Condiments*

Sun-dried Tomatoes   63

Candy-Sweet Chopped Fresh Tomatoes   65

Salt-cured Nasturtium Buds   66

DESSERTS AND GELATO

Rose-scented Custard   67

My Ricotta Dessert   68

Meyer Lemon Gelato Topped with Fresh Figs and Pistachios   69

Mint Gelato Topped with Shavings of Darkest Chocolate   71

Meyer Lemon Granita   73

• Summer Garden •

Basilico foglia di lattuga • lettuce-leaf basil

Basilico Genovese • Genoa basil

Borragine • borage leaves and flowers

Citronella • lemon verbena

Fagioli rampicante • green beans

Finocchio selvatico • wild fennel

Gelsomino • jasmine blossoms

Jimmy Nardello's sweet Italian frying pepper

Limone • lemons, blossoms, and leaves

Menta • mint

Mentuccia/nepitella • wild mint

Nasturzio • nasturtium leaves, flowers, and buds

Origano • Italian oregano

Pomodoro Costoluto Genovese • Genoa tomato

Pomodoro Principe Borghese • Principe Borghese tomato

Pomodoro San Marzano • San Marzano tomato

Prezzemolo gigante di Napoli • large flat-leaf Neapolitan parsley

Ravanelli • radishes

Rosa • rose petals

Rosmarino • rosemary leaves and flowers

Rucola selvatica • wild arugula leaves and flowers

Salvia officinale • sage

Satureja montana • winter savory

Sungold cherry tomatoes

Zucchetta serpente di Sicilia • snakelike Sicilian zucchini, leaves, and male flowers

Zucchino striato d'Italia • striated Italian zucchini, leaves, and male flowers

FRESH RICOTTA WITH BASIL AND PARSLEY

Serves 8 to 10

What pure pleasure to assemble this sweetly herbal yet tangy spread with its sneaky touch of not-too-hot minced fresh green chile and coarsely ground black pepper.

1 pound whole-milk ricotta
$1/2$ cup chopped fresh basil
$1/2$ cup chopped fresh flat-leaf parsley
$1/4$ teaspoon minced mildly hot fresh green chile
Sea salt
Extra virgin olive oil
Coarsely ground black pepper

COMBINE the ricotta, basil, parsley, and chile in a bowl. Stir to distribute ingredients evenly. Add salt to taste. Cover and refrigerate for at least 30 minutes.

REMOVE from the refrigerator and bring to room temperature before serving. Transfer to a serving plate and shape into a dome. Drizzle with olive oil and grind black pepper over the top.

SERVE with crostini and place a cruet of olive oil and a pepper grinder on the table. Refrigerate any leftover ricotta mixture for up to 1 day.

LA BARONESSA'S ROSES

Serves 8

The "Baronessa" side of my personality is reflected in this special offering. Inspired by the beauty of roses, the assembled dish resembles fantasy flowers.

If possible, use *foglia di lattuga* basil, literally "lettuce leaf" basil. It has very large leaves and is exceptionally aromatic. Otherwise, seek out the largest basil leaves available and increase the number.

> 8 *foglia di lattuga* basil leaves or 16 large basil leaves from the market (or as many as needed to cover the mozzarella balls)
> 8 bocconcini (small mozzarella balls), drained
> Sea salt
> Extra virgin olive oil
> 8 long, thin slices Parma prosciutto (about 10 inches or more in length)

BRING a small pot of water to a boil, then take it off the heat. Have a bowl of cold water nearby. One leaf at a time, dip the basil in the hot water just long enough to soften the leaf and set the color, about 5 seconds. Immediately dip in the bowl of cold water. Gently pat the leaves dry on a dishtowel.

Lightly **SEASON** the mozzarella rounds with salt to taste and wrap each basil leaf around the cheese. The basil will adhere to the cheese to form a neat green packet.

PLACE a little olive oil in a small bowl. Roll each mozzarella ball in oil until the basil is glossy. Set aside.

On individual plates, using one slice of prosciutto, start to **FORM** a rose. Begin at the center of the "rose," forming a tight bud shape, and continue circling around to create a large blossom, always gathering it close at the base. Place a mozzarella ball at the center of each prosciutto rose. Serve immediately.

You can prepare the bocconcini an hour in advance and leave them at room temperature; they will still retain the bright green color of the basil. The "rose," however, must be formed just before serving or the prosciutto will dry out.

TINY HERB FRITTATAS

Makes 24 miniature frittatas

This charming dish is a series of miniature frittatas, each featuring one herb—a wonderful way to appreciate the flavor of a single herb and a way to showcase all the different herbs growing in your garden. If your herb garden boasts twenty-four herbs, try a different one in each little frittata. I call for eight of the most widely used herbs in Italian cooking.

Serve the frittatas as part of an offering of antipasti, as a first course, or as a light main dish. Sprigs of fresh herbs and chive blossoms, dandelion blossoms, or nasturtiums would make a lovely and appropriate garnish, further enhancing the herbal aromas and visual pleasure.

Butter for greasing muffin tin, at room temperature

6 large eggs

$1/4$ cup whole milk

Pinch of sea salt

$1/4$ cup freshly grated Parmigiano-Reggiano cheese, plus extra for sprinkling

$1^1/2$ teaspoons finely chopped fresh thyme

$1^1/2$ teaspoons finely chopped fresh flat-leaf parsley

$1^1/2$ teaspoons finely chopped fresh basil

$1^1/2$ teaspoons snipped fresh chives

$1^1/2$ teaspoons finely chopped fresh spearmint

$3/4$ teaspoon finely chopped fresh rosemary tips

$1^1/2$ teaspoons finely chopped fresh sage

$1^1/2$ teaspoons finely chopped fresh oregano

PREHEAT the oven to 350°F. Lightly butter a nonstick (preferably silicone) 24-cup miniature muffin pan.

COMBINE the eggs, milk, and salt in a bowl and gently beat with a fork until well combined. Add the Parmesan and beat with a fork until incorporated.

POUR the egg mixture into a 1-quart measuring cup with a pouring spout. Carefully distribute the batter equally among the muffin cups, with approximately 1 tablespoon in each one. Sprinkle a small amount of one herb over each frittata and use a thin wooden skewer to stir the herb into the egg mixture. If using the herbs listed here, you will have 3 frittatas for each herb. Sprinkle a little Parmesan over the top of each frittata.

PLACE the muffin pan in the oven for 3 to 4 minutes, or until the frittatas puff up slightly and are tender but hold their shape. Let cool briefly, then slip the frittatas out of the pan. Serve immediately.

RICOTTA AND CAPRINO LAYERED WITH FRESH BASIL LEAVES

Serves 6 as a first course or 12 as part of a buffet

Creamy ricotta combined with the lemony tang of caprino, fresh goat cheese, is simply layered with whole basil leaves and drizzled with extra virgin olive oil to produce a light and aromatic spread. I've always loved light, fresh cheeses. And using whole basil leaves instead of pesto infuses the cheese mixture with basil's flavor and perfume without overwhelming the fresh cheese.

Serve the spread with the tender, white inner stalks of celery with the leaves still attached (the leaves are not only delicious but also have health-enhancing qualities), leaves of Treviso radicchio if available, and long grissini—all perfect for dipping into the layers to scoop out a bit of the fragrant spread.

$^1/_2$ pound whole-milk ricotta, at room temperature
$^1/_2$ pound fresh goat cheese, at room temperature
Fruity extra virgin olive oil
Big handful of fresh basil leaves, reserving a few for garnish
Sea salt
Coarsely ground black pepper
Celery sticks, radicchio leaves, and grissini (breadsticks)

COMBINE the ricotta and goat cheese in a bowl. Stir with a wooden spoon to blend thoroughly. Divide into three portions. Lightly oil a glass loaf pan large enough to hold all the cheese. Pack one-third of the cheese mixture into the bottom of the pan and smooth the top with the back of a large spoon. Cover with a layer of basil leaves and press them into the cheese so they stay in place. Drizzle with 1 or 2 tablespoons olive oil. Season with salt and pepper to taste.

SPREAD another third of the cheese mixture over the basil, attempting to keep the leaves intact. Press another layer of basil leaves into the cheese and again season with olive oil, salt, and pepper.

MAKE a final layer of cheese and spread it evenly. Drizzle with olive oil and season with salt and pepper. Press a piece of parchment paper directly over the cheese to prevent the top from drying out.

If serving within an hour, **LEAVE** the "torta" out at room temperature. If making it in advance, refrigerate and then bring back to room temperature. Serve directly from the loaf pan, garnished with basil leaves. Or, invert the loaf onto a flat serving platter and garnish with basil leaves. With either method of serving, surround the spread with celery sticks, radicchio leaves, and grissini.

HARD-COOKED EGGS WRAPPED IN GIANT BASIL LEAVES

Serves 6

Chickens that roam freely and are fed organically produce eggs with high nutritional value. You will be amazed at the intense saffron-gold color of the yolk, proof of its superior quality.

The eggs cook until the yolks are firm but moist. They provide an excellent opportunity to use the large *foglia di lattuga* (lettuce-leaf) basil leaves as wrappers. Eggs wrapped in basil leaves make for perfect picnic food. Just pack some oil-cured black olives, a loaf of rustic bread, and a cold bottle of crisp white wine.

> 6 large eggs
> Sea salt
> 6 *foglia di lattuga* basil leaves or enough smaller leaves
>   to wrap the eggs completely
> Freshly ground black pepper
> Extra virgin olive oil

In a medium saucepan, gently **IMMERSE** the eggs in water to cover by about 1 inch. Slowly bring the water to a gentle boil. Cook for about 9 minutes, carefully stirring the eggs around in the water to set the yolks in the center of each egg.

DRAIN and place the pot under cold running water until the eggs are cool to the touch. With the eggs still immersed in cool water, gently crack the exterior of the shell until the entire shell forms a crackle pattern. Keeping the eggs under water, carefully peel each egg, removing the thin membrane. Let the eggs dry on a clean dishtowel.

Meanwhile, bring a small pot of salted water to a boil and **BLANCH** the basil leaves for 1 or 2 seconds, just until they become bright green and pliable. Carefully remove the leaves from the water and pat dry, leaving them a bit moist. This helps the basil adhere to the egg.

CUT the eggs in half lengthwise. Season each half with salt and pepper to taste and moisten both sides with olive oil. Press the halves together to create the appearance of a whole egg.

ENFOLD each egg in a basil leaf, overlapping the leaf to form a seal. Wrap each egg in parchment paper. Gather the paper at the top and tie with a bit of kitchen twine. Refrigerate until ready to take on a picnic, or pack your basket and enjoy a simple but exquisite meal outdoors.

MEYER LEMON AND CUCUMBER SALAD WITH MINT

Serves 4

Meyer lemons are incredibly sweet. When they are left on the tree to ripen fully, some people mistake them for oranges since they become a golden color, very different from the yellow coloring of Eureka lemons, those most commonly found in markets. When sliced thin, as they are in this salad, the entire lemon is not only edible, but delicious and refreshing.

1 tablespoon finely diced red onion

1 large Meyer lemon, cut into thin slices

$^1/_2$ medium cucumber, peeled and sliced into about $^1/_8$-inch rounds

18 small fresh mint leaves, torn

Best-quality extra virgin olive oil

Sea salt

Coarsely ground black pepper

To extract bitterness, **PLACE** the onion in a small bowl and cover with cold water. Change the water every 20 minutes until the onion is sweet. Drain well and dry on a paper towel.

PLACE the lemon and cucumber slices, onion, and mint leaves on a serving platter, and drizzle with olive oil. Very gently toss the ingredients in enough oil to moisten the salad generously. Add salt and pepper to taste and toss again.

ARRANGE the salad so that the lemon and cucumber slices overlap slightly. Let rest for about 5 minutes for flavors to mingle. This salad is especially nice served before or after a meal featuring grilled fish or even with the main course, plated alongside the seafood.

ZUCCHINI CARPACCIO WITH ALMONDS

Serves 4

Everyone is familiar with raw beef carpaccio. Zucchini carpaccio uses the same technique to create paper-thin slices and tops the zucchini shavings with ingredients that bring out the sweet vegetal flavor of this vigorous grower.

I've used several different varieties of zucchini when I prepare this dish. Most important is to pick the zucchini when small and sweet, without noticeably developed seeds.

$\frac{1}{2}$ cup whole almonds
4 small, very firm zucchini, preferably just picked, ends trimmed
Extra virgin olive oil
Sea salt
Parmigiano-Reggiano cheese

PREHEAT the oven to 375°F.

SPREAD the almonds on a baking sheet and toast for approximately 10 minutes. Remove from the oven and let cool.

SELECT a large oval platter, preferably white. Use a mandoline or a wide vegetable peeler to make long shavings of zucchini. Spread the zucchini on the platter, drizzle with olive oil, and sprinkle very lightly with salt.

Working over the zucchini with a standard vegetable peeler, **SHAVE** enough Parmesan to lightly cover the zucchini.

Coarsely **CHOP** the almonds and distribute evenly over the cheese. Immediately before serving, embellish with an additional very light drizzling of olive oil.

SUMMER CAPRESE

Serves 4

The original caprese, by now well known in America, is one of the great dishes of summer when properly made. *Caprese* refers to Capri, where the salad originated.

I use two of my Italian heirloom tomatoes in this version, real buffalo mozzarella, and the two herbs that are the essence of summer in Italy—fresh basil and aromatic dried oregano.

Nowadays, most mozzarella in Italy is made from cow's milk. It's called *fior di latte* mozzarella. But the true mozzarella produced in Campania is made from water buffalo milk, the original ingredient in insalata caprese.

4 large fresh mozzarella balls

2 Costoluto Genovese tomatoes or other large vine-ripened variety

4 Principe Borghese tomatoes or other medium vine-ripened variety

Handful of Sungold or other small, sweet cherry tomatoes

Sea salt

6 to 8 tablespoons extra virgin olive oil

2 teaspoons home-dried Italian oregano (page 64)

Handful of just-picked basil leaves

SLICE the mozzarella into ¼-inch-thick rounds. If very moist, drain on kitchen towels.

SLICE the larger tomatoes into ¼-inch-thick rounds. Cut the cherry tomatoes in half.

ARRANGE the mozzarella slices in a slightly overlapping pattern on a large serving dish. Season with salt and 4 tablespoons of the olive oil.

ARRANGE the tomato slices over the cheese, alternating the different varieties. Sprinkle the halved cherry tomatoes over the top. Drizzle with additional olive oil to taste and season with salt. Sprinkle the oregano over the tomatoes.

WIPE the basil leaves clean with a damp kitchen towel. Tear the leaves into fragments and scatter over the top. Serve immediately.

PARSLEY AND RICE SALAD

Serves 4 to 6

Given the right conditions, parsley grows like wildfire in the garden. And, as with many edible plants and herbs, the more you pick, the more the plant produces.

Use either type of parsley, the large flat-leaf Neapolitan variety or the smaller, feathery, more common flat-leaf parsley.

Jimmy Nardello's pepper is piquant but not hot. I don't know who Jimmy is, but I love his peppers.

1 cup Arborio rice

Sea salt

6 tablespoons extra virgin olive oil

2 cups tightly packed fresh flat-leaf parsley leaves

1/2 cup pitted oil-cured black olives, coarsely chopped

1 tablespoon finely minced Jimmy Nardello's sweet Italian frying pepper
    or a mildly hot fresh green chile

Meyer lemon wedges

COOK the rice in abundant boiling salted water for about 16 minutes, or until al dente. Drain well.

PLACE the rice in a shallow serving dish; toss with 4 tablespoons of the olive oil and salt to taste. Let cool to room temperature.

CHOP the parsley medium-fine and toss with the rice until evenly distributed. Add the olives and pepper and toss again. Drizzle the remaining 2 tablespoons olive oil over the top and stir gently. Taste and add salt if needed.

SERVE with Meyer lemon wedges on the side for each person to squeeze over the salad. (Adding lemon in advance discolors the parsley. Freshly squeezing the lemon also keeps the perfume of the lemon vibrant.)

AVOCADO ON THE HALF-SHELL

Serves 4

Here, avocados are served cool, fragrant with herbs warmed in the hot summer sun.
Serve on a sultry summer night accompanied by a chilled bottle of Italian white wine.

2 large Hass avocados, ripe but firm (the flesh should be bright green with no
     blemishes or bruises), lightly chilled
1 small Meyer lemon
$^1/_4$ cup extra virgin olive oil
Handful of fresh basil leaves, coarsely chopped
Handful of fresh mint leaves, coarsely chopped
Sea salt
$^1/_4$ cup almonds, toasted (see page 29) and coarsely chopped
Sungold cherry tomato clusters or other small, sweet cherry tomatoes on the vine

Carefully **CUT** the avocados in half without removing the peel. Gently twist to separate the halves. Insert a sharp paring knife into the pit and pop it out. Immediately
squeeze lemon juice over the exposed avocado flesh. If necessary, cut a small slice off
the bottom of each avocado half to stabilize it.

In a small bowl, **COMBINE** the olive oil, basil, and mint. Season with salt. Add fresh
lemon juice to taste to the olive oil and herb mixture.

SPOON the herbal dressing into the cavities of the avocados. Distribute the almonds
over the top and drape a small cluster of tomatoes on each avocado.

SOUP WITH NEW POTATOES, SAFFRON, BASIL, AND MASCARPONE

Serves 4

In this soup, the humble potato becomes quite sophisticated with the addition of saffron, mascarpone cheese, and fresh basil.

2 tablespoons extra virgin olive oil
2 tablespoons unsalted butter
$^1/_2$ medium onion, finely chopped
Sea salt
8 small Yukon gold potatoes
Generous pinch of saffron threads
$^1/_4$ cup mascarpone cheese
About $^1/_4$ cup slivered fresh basil
Freshly grated Parmigiano-Reggiano cheese

PLACE the olive oil, butter, and onion in a medium saucepan over low heat. Sauté until the onion is meltingly tender.

Meanwhile, **BRING** a pot of salted water to a boil and cook the whole potatoes until tender. Drain and, when cool enough to handle, peel the potatoes.

ADD the potatoes to the saucepan with the onion. Crumble the saffron threads into the saucepan. Over low heat, toss the mixture. Add 2 cups water and simmer for about 15 minutes. Use a potato masher or a wooden spoon to create a coarse puree. Add salt to taste.

BRING back to a simmer and add a little water as needed to thin the puree if too dense. Remove from heat and stir in the mascarpone. Ladle the soup into serving bowls and sprinkle with basil and Parmesan.

BARLEY SOUP WITH SUMMER HERBS

Serves 4

Barley has a texture that is irresistible—chewy and satisfying. It is usually a part of cold-weather soups. Here, I've turned this grain into a summery soup that is bright green with herbs and dotted with golden tomato.

 3 tablespoons extra virgin olive oil
 2 garlic cloves, chopped
 Handful of fresh flat-leaf parsley, chopped
 2 teaspoons chopped fresh oregano
 2 cups cooked barley
 About 6 cups vegetable broth or water
 Sea salt
 1 cup Sungold or other small, sweet cherry tomatoes
 Handful of fresh basil leaves, torn into fragments

PLACE the olive oil and garlic in a soup pot and cook over low heat until the garlic is tender, 2 to 3 minutes. Add the parsley and oregano and let warm, stirring often over low heat for about 5 minutes.

ADD the barley to the pot and enough broth to cover generously. Season with salt to taste.

COOK at a gentle simmer for 10 minutes, adding the tomatoes in the final few minutes of cooking.

Before serving, **TASTE** for salt and sprinkle with basil.

SPAGHETTINI WITH BASIL LEAVES AND STRANDS OF LEMON ZEST

Serves 4 to 6

Fresh basil, more than any herb, suffers greatly when it must be transported to the market. The supermarket misting mechanism that sprays water on produce and unsuspecting customers has a disastrous effect on fresh basil. The natural moisture contained within its leaves keeps them bright and lively and enhances their sweet perfume, but the leaves droop and discolor under the weight of all that misting. When basil is sold in plastic containers, it becomes crushed, causing bruising and deterioration of quality.

Basil is among the tenderest of leaves in the garden, perhaps the most tender. If there is only one herb you can grow on your terrace or sunny windowsill, let it be basil.

Sea salt
1 pound imported spaghettini
6 tablespoons extra virgin olive oil
3 garlic cloves, finely chopped
Large handful of fresh basil leaves
1/2 Meyer lemon, zested in long strands, using a zester

BRING a large pot of salted water to a boil; cook the spaghettini until al dente.

Meanwhile, PLACE the olive oil and garlic in a large sauté pan. Over very low heat, warm the garlic for 3 to 4 minutes. Toss in the basil and stir gently to coat the leaves lightly.

DRAIN the spaghettini and toss gently with the basil and olive oil, being careful not to bruise the leaves, and add salt to taste. Sprinkle with the lemon zest and stir once or twice. Serve immediately.

SPAGHETTI WITH TOMATO SAUCE AND FRESH BASIL LEAVES

Serves 4

My pot of basil provides me with fresh leaves all summer long. I feel fortunate to be able to make this simple but highly aromatic pasta with fresh-plucked sprigs.

  $^1/_4$ cup extra virgin olive oil
  2 tablespoons unsalted butter
  1 onion, finely diced
  2 pounds assorted garden tomatoes, peeled and seeded
  10 fresh basil leaves, plus 4 small sprigs basil
  Sea salt
  Freshly ground black pepper
  1 pound imported spaghetti

In a large sauté pan, **COMBINE** the olive oil, butter, and onion. Cook over low heat until the onion is soft and translucent, about 10 minutes.

ADD the tomatoes, basil leaves, and salt and pepper to taste. Use a wooden spoon to crush the tomatoes, which will break down quickly into a sauce. Simmer for about 10 minutes, stirring every so often.

Meanwhile, **BRING** a large pot of salted water to a boil and cook the spaghetti until al dente.

TOSS the spaghetti with the sauce and serve immediately, garnishing each serving with a small sprig of basil.

ORECCHIETTE WITH LITTLE YELLOW TOMATOES AND PARSLEY

Serves 4

My Sungold cherry tomato plant keeps producing the sweetest little golden tomatoes for months. Since the tomatoes are small, they pair nicely with orecchiette, landing neatly into the pasta shape's small bowls. When you take a bite, the tomatoes burst in your mouth and release their sweet juices.

> 1/4 cup extra virgin olive oil, plus extra as needed
>
> 2 garlic cloves, finely chopped
>
> 2 cups Sungold or other small, sweet cherry tomatoes
>
> Sea salt
>
> 1 pound imported orecchiette
>
> 1/4 cup coarsely chopped fresh flat-leaf parsley
>
> Ricotta salata

PLACE the olive oil and garlic in a large sauté pan and warm over low heat for about 5 minutes. Add the whole cherry tomatoes and salt to taste. Cook over low heat for 4 minutes, stirring gently to coat the tomatoes without crushing them.

Meanwhile, BRING a large pot of salted water to a boil and cook the orecchiette until tender but slightly al dente. Drain.

Just before the pasta is ready, STIR the parsley into the tomatoes. Carefully toss the tomato mixture with the pasta. Add more olive oil and salt as needed so the pasta is glossy. Shave ricotta salata over the top and serve.

TUBETTI LA FAVORITA

Serves 4

This is a true summer pasta. A tradition in Italy is to combine fresh diced tomatoes, seasoned with garlic and basil, with hot pasta for a refreshing dish. The heat of the pasta slightly "cooks" the other ingredients and causes a glorious explosion of scents.

Once you have diced a variety of tomatoes, a red onion, and celery, and slivered the basil, all that is required is cooking the pasta. Serve in the garden to enjoy the pasta *all'aperto* (outdoors).

1 cup seeded and diced assorted garden tomatoes
$^1\!/_2$ cup finely diced red onion
$^1\!/_2$ cup finely diced tender celery stalks, including leaves
$^1\!/_2$ cup extra virgin olive oil
Sea salt
1 pound imported tubetti
Freshly ground black pepper
$^1\!/_2$ cup slivered fresh basil

In a large pasta serving bowl, **COMBINE** the tomato, onion, and celery. Mix with ¼ cup of the olive oil and season with salt to taste. Set aside for up to 1 hour.

BRING a large pot of salted water to a boil and cook the tubetti until al dente. Drain and stir the hot pasta into the vegetable mixture. Add the remaining olive oil and salt and pepper to taste.

Just before serving, **SPRINKLE** the basil over the top, and then toss at the table.

PASTA WITH ALMOST EVERY HERB IN THE GARDEN

Serves 4 to 6

I've made this sauce in Italy with wild herbs that I gathered in the countryside. I love preparing it with my own fresh herbs. Wild herbs are quite pungent and highly aromatic, and a little goes a long way. When I make this pasta from my garden, I use a wide variety of herbs to create the complex taste and aroma of truly wild herbs and achieve a very successful dish. Feel free to use whatever assortment of herbs appeals to you or is available to you.

Sea salt
1 pound imported orecchiette or penne rigate
6 tablespoons extra virgin olive oil, plus extra for serving
3 garlic cloves, finely chopped
$^1/_4$ teaspoon hot red pepper flakes
2 fresh bay leaves, torn in half
2 teaspoons chopped fresh thyme
2 teaspoons chopped fresh rosemary
2 teaspoons chopped fresh winter savory
1 tablespoon chopped fresh oregano
1 teaspoon chopped fresh marjoram
2 tablespoons chopped fresh mint
3 tablespoons finely chopped wild fennel tops
Large handful of arugula, stemmed and chopped
1 heaping tablespoon salt-cured capers or Salt-cured Nasturtium Buds (page 66)
Freshly grated pecorino cheese

BRING a large pot of salted water to a boil and cook the pasta until al dente.

(continued)

Meanwhile, **PLACE** the olive oil in a large sauté pan. Add the garlic and red pepper and warm over low heat until the garlic is tender, 2 to 3 minutes. Add all the herbs, the capers, and salt to taste and stir gently. Let the herbs warm over low heat for 8 to 10 minutes, at which time the sauce should be quite aromatic.

DRAIN the pasta and, off the heat, toss with the sauce, adding more olive oil as needed. Serve sprinkled with a few spoonfuls of pecorino.

RISOTTO WITH ZUCCHINO STRIATO D'ITALIA

Serves 4

The zucchini in the garden beckons. When cooked in a risotto, the zucchini breaks down, becoming sweet and creamy, and merging with the rice.

1/4 cup plus 2 tablespoons extra virgin olive oil

1/2 onion, finely diced

2 striato d'Italia or other medium zucchini, diced

2 garlic cloves, finely chopped

2 cups Arborio rice

6 cups vegetable broth or water, brought to a simmer

8 fresh basil leaves, cut into thin slivers

Sea salt

Freshly ground black pepper

1/2 cup freshly grated Grana Padano cheese

HEAT the 1/4 cup olive oil in a heavy-bottomed 2-quart saucepan over low heat. Add the onion and sauté slowly until soft. Add the zucchini and garlic, and briefly sauté over moderate heat, 2 to 3 minutes. Add the rice and stir until the rice is translucent, 1 to 2 minutes.

ADD the hot broth to the rice mixture one ladleful at a time, stirring frequently. The rice should cook very slowly over low heat. Wait until the liquid is absorbed before adding the next ladleful of broth. Midway during cooking, add the basil and salt and pepper to taste.

When the risotto is al dente, **ADD** the remaining 2 tablespoons olive oil and the cheese. Turn off the heat and stir briefly to combine. Serve immediately.

RISOTTO VERDE

Serves 4

This risotto pays tribute to one of the greatest but all-too-often undervalued herbs in the garden.

¼ cup extra virgin olive oil
3 or 4 salt-cured anchovy fillets, scraped of excess salt, coarsely chopped
1 cup chopped fresh flat-leaf parsley
4 garlic cloves, chopped
Sea salt
Freshly ground black pepper
½ cup dry white wine
2 cups Arborio rice
6 cups meat broth or water, brought to a simmer
Freshly grated pecorino cheese (optional)

In a medium, heavy-bottomed saucepan, **PLACE** the olive oil and anchovies and cook over low heat, about 6 minutes. Add ¼ cup of the parsley and the garlic and cook for another 2 minutes. Season with salt and pepper to taste. Add the wine, raise the heat, and let the wine evaporate completely. Lower the heat and add the rice. Stir to coat the grains.

ADD enough broth to just cover the rice. Cook at a simmer, stirring frequently, until the liquid is absorbed. Continue adding the liquid, always just enough to cover, until the rice is al dente and the risotto is creamy. Add the remaining ¾ cup parsley during the final 5 minutes of cooking. Turn off the heat. Cover and let the risotto rest for a minute.

SERVE in shallow pasta bowls with grated pecorino cheese at the table, if desired.

BREAD "LASAGNA"

Serves 6

A more rustic or hearty dish would be hard to come by. Bread lasagna resembles traditional lasagna in only one way—the ingredients are layered. Instead of sheets of fresh pasta, slices of dry bread are interspersed with tomato sauce, herbs, and cheeses.

Bread lasagna is very easy to prepare, especially compared to typical lasagna. It makes use of dried country bread. It can be prepared in a larger baking dish to serve a big group of hungry friends. Don't worry about precise amounts of each ingredient. This is a no-fail dish that everyone will love.

1-pound loaf of rustic, day-old bread

$^1/_2$ cup plus 3 tablespoons extra virgin olive oil, plus extra for the dish

2 garlic cloves, chopped

$^3/_4$ cup chopped fresh flat-leaf parsley

2 cups peeled coarsely chopped garden tomatoes

$1^1/_2$ teaspoons dried oregano

$^1/_2$ cup freshly grated pecorino cheese

4 ounces sliced fontina cheese

1 to $1^1/_2$ cups mild beef broth or water

PREHEAT the oven to 200°F. Cut the bread into ½-inch slices and set them on a baking sheet. Depending on the freshness of the bread, bake for 30 to 45 minutes. Just dry the bread; do not allow it to color. Remove from the oven and raise the heat to 375°F.

HEAT the 3 tablespoons of olive oil, the garlic, and ½ cup of the parsley over medium heat until fragrant, about 5 minutes. Add the tomatoes with their juice and simmer for 15 minutes, breaking down the tomatoes with a wooden spoon. The sauce should be chunky and glossy.

(continued)

SPREAD enough olive oil to coat an 8-inch square gratin dish or equivalent. Evenly distribute ⅓ cup of the tomato sauce. Layer slices of bread on top of the tomato sauce. Drizzle with 2 tablespoons of the olive oil and sprinkle with ½ teaspoon of the oregano and a tablespoon of the parsley.

SPREAD a third of the remaining tomato sauce over the bread and drizzle with 2 tablespoons of the olive oil. Sprinkle on a heaping tablespoon of pecorino and layer half of the fontina.

REPEAT the steps, starting with the bread. Add a final layer of bread and the remaining tomato sauce. Add 1 to 1½ cups of broth or water to moisten the layers, depending on how dry your bread is. Sprinkle the remaining ½ teaspoon dried oregano, the rest of the parsley, and the remaining pecorino on top. Drizzle with the rest of the olive oil.

COVER and bake for 45 minutes. Uncover and cook for 15 more minutes. Let rest at least 10 minutes before serving.

POTATO, OLIVE, AND RICOTTA TORTA

Serves 6

This satisfying main dish is amazingly simple to assemble. The torta can be served warm, accompanied by a tomato and basil salad. Or cut it into smaller pieces and serve as an antipasto.

2 tablespoons extra virgin olive oil, plus extra for oiling the dish

1 tablespoon chopped fresh flat-leaf parsley

1 teaspoon chopped fresh rosemary

1 teaspoon chopped fresh sage

1 teaspoon chopped fresh thyme

$^1/_2$ pound Yukon gold potatoes, peeled, diced, and boiled in salted water until tender

4 large eggs

$^3/_4$ pound whole-milk ricotta

$^1/_4$ cup pitted oil-cured black olives, coarsely chopped

$^1/_2$ cup freshly grated pecorino cheese

Unsalted butter

Dried bread crumbs

PREHEAT the oven to 375°F degrees. Oil a gratin dish just large enough to hold the ingredients, about 3 inches deep.

HEAT the olive oil with the herbs in a saucepan over low heat until fragrant. Add the potatoes and stir to coat with the oil for 1 to 2 minutes. Mash the mixture and let cool.

MIX the eggs and ricotta until well combined. Add the potatoes, olives, and pecorino and stir.

(continued)

TRANSFER the mixture to the prepared dish. Dot with butter and sprinkle bread crumbs on top.

BAKE the torta for 45 minutes, or until firm and light golden. Serve warm or at room temperature.

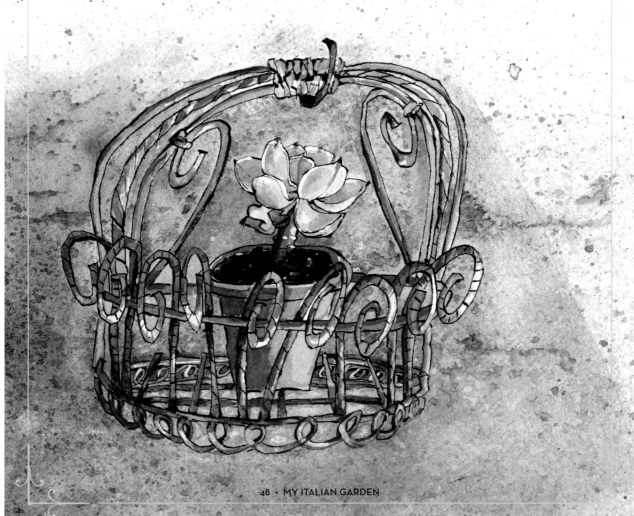

ROLLED THIN FRITTATA FILLED WITH RICOTTA AND PARSLEY

Serves 4

Italians look to eggs for nutrition—but not in the morning. Frittatas are served as a light lunch or supper, or as part of an assortment of antipasti.

Serve these rolled frittatas with a tomato and basil salad or an *insalata mista* with lettuces, tomato, cucumber, and one or two other crisp, raw garden vegetables.

8 large eggs, lightly beaten
Sea salt
Freshly ground black pepper
3 to 4 tablespoons freshly grated pecorino Romano cheese
Extra virgin olive oil
1 pound whole-milk ricotta, drained
1/2 cup chopped fresh flat-leaf parsley

PREHEAT the oven to 200°F.

In a bowl **COMBINE** the eggs, salt and pepper to taste, and pecorino. Beat together with a fork.

Lightly **COAT** the bottom of a medium skillet with olive oil and set over medium-high heat. When the oil is hot, add one-fourth of the egg mixture or enough to produce a thin pancake. Swirl the pan to distribute the egg mixture evenly. Reduce the heat and cook until the frittata is just firm. Flip the frittata and lightly cook it on the other side. Transfer to a plate. Quickly make the remaining frittatas.

WARM the ricotta in a sauté pan over very low heat. Add the parsley and season with salt and pepper to taste. Divide the ricotta among the frittatas, mounding it in a cigar

shape near the edge of one side. Roll them up loosely, place in a baking dish, and keep warm in the oven until ready to serve.

REMOVE the frittatas from the oven and serve warm.

FRITTATA FIORITA

Serves 4

Scientific research into the health-giving properties of plants is still in its infancy. Vegetables and herbs contain not only an amazing array of vitamins and minerals but also antiviral and other disease-fighting elements. The flowers of plants also contain essences that are powerful agents of health and healing, although their beauty and scents might seem reward enough.

6 to 8 large eggs
Sea salt
1 cup assorted flowers, such as nasturtium petals and arugula, oregano, and
    rosemary, plus a few for garnish
$^{1}/_{2}$ cup freshly grated Grana Padano cheese
2 tablespoons unsalted butter

PREHEAT the broiler.

BREAK the eggs into a bowl and beat them lightly with a fork. Add the salt, blossoms, and cheese, and stir.

PLACE the butter in a large ovenproof sauté pan and set over medium-high heat. Add the egg mixture and lower the heat. Cook the frittata slowly, stirring the eggs until large curds form. Stop stirring and cook until the frittata is firm except for the top.

FINISH cooking the top by placing the frittata under the broiler (or in a preheated 400°F oven) until the top is just set. Let it cool in the pan for 1 to 2 minutes. Place a serving plate over the top of the pan and invert the frittata on it. Garnish with fresh flowers.

GREEN BEANS WITH EUROPEAN-STYLE BUTTER AND BASIL LEAVES

Serves 4

It is a pleasure to go into the garden with a colander and search for young green beans among the leafy vines. Garden green beans cook quickly and taste very sweet. European or European-style butter is creamier than our regular butter. Look for it in markets. Its extra richness makes the green beans luscious.

Sea salt
1 pound green beans
3 to 4 tablespoons imported or European-style unsalted butter
Handful of small fresh basil leaves

BRING a pot of salted water to a boil and cook the beans for about 5 minutes, or until al dente. Drain.

In a large sauté pan, **MELT** the butter over low heat. Add the beans and gently turn them in the butter several times until they are glossy. Cook over very low heat until the beans have absorbed the butter and just a bit of buttery liquid remains.

REMOVE from heat, stir in the basil leaves, and let rest for a few minutes to allow the basil to perfume the beans.

LITTLE GOLDEN TOMATOES SAUTÉED WITH GREEN AND BLACK OLIVES AND PARSLEY

Serves 4 to 6

This simple recipe is a wonderful addition to your repertoire of summer vegetable dishes. The sweet tomatoes and pungent flavor of olives, both oil-cured black ones and brined green olives, wake up any appetite. This dish goes well with grilled fish or meats to round out a summer meal eaten under the shade of a big umbrella. It is also good tossed with short pasta and served hot or at room temperature.

3 tablespoons extra virgin olive oil
1 garlic clove, coarsely chopped
$^1\!/_2$ cup coarsely chopped fresh flat-leaf parsley
$2^1\!/_2$ cups Sungold or other small, sweet cherry tomatoes
8 oil-cured black olives, pitted and coarsely chopped
6 Sicilian green olives, pitted and coarsely chopped
Sea salt (optional)

PLACE the olive oil in a medium sauté pan over low heat. Add the garlic and parsley and cook for 2 to 3 minutes, or until fragrant and glossy. Add the tomatoes and stir 2 to 3 minutes until the tomatoes are glossy and the parsley is evenly distributed. Stir in the olives and season with a little salt if needed. Stir gently with a wooden spoon until the tomatoes are warm through but intact. Serve warm or at room temperature.

SICILIAN ZUCCHINI AL PICCHI PACCHI

Serves 4

The first time I tasted this unusual summer squash, I was twelve years old and seated at the dining table of relatives in Palermo. I remember thinking I'd never seen such soaring ceilings before. The heat outside meant the shutters were closed, so we ate in half-light. The zucchini was very sweet, lightly cooked in just a little water, salt, and a touch of garlic.

I've added a few of my garden's Principe Borghese tomatoes and freshest basil. "Quick cooking" is the translation of *picchi pacchi,* usually a tomato and basil sauce.

$^1/_4$ cup extra virgin olive oil
1 onion, finely diced
4 cups zucchetta serpente di Sicilia or other zucchini, cut into 1-inch dice
Sea salt
Freshly ground black pepper
2 Principe Borghese or other vine-ripened tomatoes, peeled, seeded,
    and coarsely chopped
Handful of fresh basil leaves

PLACE the olive oil and onion in a medium sauté pàn. Sauté over low heat until the onion turns light gold. Add the zucchini and salt and pepper to taste. Stir and cook for about 5 minutes. Add the tomatoes and additional salt and pepper to taste. Cook over medium-low heat until the zucchini is just tender and the tomatoes have turned into a light sauce. Just before serving, tear the basil leaves into fragments and sprinkle over the top.

MUSHROOMS AND BREAD SLICES ON
ROSEMARY BRANCH SKEWERS

Serves 2

Using rosemary branches as skewers perfumes the air as well as the mushrooms and bread as they grill. It is preferable to use a wood-fired grill, which imparts yet another dimension—a natural smoky flavor.

6 large cremini or portobello mushrooms, about 2 inches in diameter

8 slices rustic baguette, about the same size as the mushrooms

3 tablespoons extra virgin olive oil, plus extra for brushing on assembled skewers

2 garlic cloves, finely chopped

1 tablespoon finely chopped fresh rosemary

1 tablespoon finely chopped fresh sage

Sea salt

Coarsely ground black pepper

2 sturdy rosemary branches, about 6 inches long, for skewers

PREHEAT the oven to 250°F. Light a wood-fired grill, if using. Trim the woody stems from the mushrooms and discard. Wipe the caps clean with a damp tea towel.

PLACE the bread slices on a baking sheet and bake for 10 minutes.

COMBINE the olive oil, garlic, rosemary, and sage in a small bowl, and season with salt and pepper. Generously stuff the mushroom caps with the oil-herb mixture. Lightly brush the mushrooms and bread with the extra olive oil.

THREAD 3 mushrooms and 4 slices of bread on each skewer, alternating the mushrooms and bread slices, starting and ending each skewer with bread. (If necessary, use

2 rosemary branches per skewer to keep the bread and mushrooms in place while turning on the grill.) Lightly brush with olive oil.

GRILL over wood coals, turning once or twice until the bread is golden. Alternatively, lightly oil a stove-top grill or preheat the broiler and oil a baking sheet. Grill or broil the skewers, turning on all sides, for about 5 minutes, or until golden brown.

PINO'S PIZZA

Makes 4 individual pizzas

My dearest friend in Italy loves this pizza and orders it every time we eat at a local pizzeria near his small town in Puglia. It isn't on the menu, but he describes it and they are happy to oblige.

>Pizza Dough (recipe follows)
>Extra virgin olive oil
>4 to 5 vine-ripened tomatoes, sliced diagonally
>Sea salt
>Pinch of hot red pepper flakes
>$^{1}/_{2}$ cup pitted, coarsely chopped green olives
>$^{1}/_{2}$ cup drained imported tuna packed in olive oil
>Handful of wild arugula, stems trimmed

When the 4 balls of dough have rested for about half an hour, **PLACE** a baking stone on the top rack of the oven and turn the heat to 500°F. Let the stone heat for at least 30 minutes.

SHAPE the pizzas, one at a time, on a lightly floured wooden peel. Use your fingertips to spread the dough into a flat, even circle about ½ inch thick. Place the dough on the back of your fist and gently stretch and rotate it, using both fists side by side. Continue stretching the dough until it is a little thicker than ¼ inch in the middle and a bit thicker around the rim, and measures about 9 inches across. Immediately after rolling out each ball, lightly spread the dough with olive oil. Arrange a quarter of the tomato slices over the top of the pizza and sprinkle with salt and red pepper. Scatter a quarter of the olives over the top and a quarter of the tuna, broken into small chunks. *(continued)*

SLIDE the pizza onto the baking stone in the oven. Bake until the edges are golden, 6 to 8 minutes, and remove from the oven. Top with arugula before serving. (You can eat the pizzas as they are made, or tent them with foil to keep them warm before serving them all at once.)

PIZZA DOUGH

Makes 4 individual pizzas

1 package (¹⁄₄ ounce) active dry yeast (not quick-rising)
About 3¹⁄₂ cups unbleached all-purpose flour, more or less as needed
3 tablespoons extra virgin olive oil, plus extra for oiling the dough
1¹⁄₂ teaspoons sea salt

PLACE ¹⁄₄ cup lukewarm water in a small bowl and sprinkle the yeast over the top. Let rest for about 5 minutes, or until it becomes a little frothy. Don't worry if no yeast action occurs as long as the expiration date is still valid.

PLACE the yeast mixture in a large mixing bowl. Add about 2 heaping cups of the flour, the olive oil, salt, and 1 cup cold water. Stir with a wooden spoon until a thick batter forms. You may have to add more flour, enough for the dough to start to pull away from the sides of the bowl.

SPRINKLE a work surface lightly with flour. Transfer the dough to the work surface. Begin kneading in the remaining flour, a little at a time, until the dough is soft and elastic. It is better to err on the side of too moist rather than too dry. Shape the dough into a ball.

Lightly **COAT** the inside of a large bowl with a very thin film of olive oil and wipe away any excess. Place the dough in the bowl and turn it over once to moisten the outside of the dough with oil. This prevents the dough from drying out as it rises. Cover tightly with plastic wrap and keep in a warm, draft-free place for about an hour. It should double in bulk.

SPRINKLE a work surface lightly with flour. Divide the dough into quarters. Roll each piece into a smooth ball, making sure to knead out any air pockets. Place the balls on the floured surface, cover with a clean cloth, and let rest for an hour.

GARDEN HERB PIZZA WITH PARMA PROSCIUTTO TOPPING

Makes 4 individual pizzas

This pizza is a study in green and pink. It features many of the summery herbs in the garden. The final *tocco*, or touch, comes when the pizza emerges from the oven. This is when you layer meltingly tender, sweet Parma prosciutto slices over the top.

> Pizza Dough (page 58)
> 3 garlic cloves, finely chopped
> ¼ cup chopped fresh flat-leaf parsley
> 3 teaspoons chopped fresh winter savory or thyme
> 2 tablespoons chopped fresh oregano
> Sea salt
> Extra virgin olive oil
> 12 slices Parma prosciutto

When the 4 balls of dough have rested for about half an hour, **PLACE** a baking stone on the top rack of the oven and turn the heat to 500°F. Let the stone heat for at least 30 minutes.

PLACE the garlic, parsley, savory, and oregano in a small bowl and stir together to distribute evenly.

PLACE a large pinch of salt on a cutting board. Put the herb and garlic mixture over the salt. With a chef's knife, finely chop the mixture until it becomes a coarsely textured puree.

SHAPE the pizzas according to the directions on page 57. Immediately after shaping each pizza, lightly brush the dough with olive oil.

SPREAD a quarter of the herb mixture over the top of each pizza without covering the thicker rim. Drizzle generously with more olive oil.

SLIDE the pizza onto the baking stone in the oven. Bake until the edges are golden, 6 to 8 minutes, and remove from the oven. Drape each pizza with 3 prosciutto slices and serve. (You can eat the pizzas as they are made, or tent them with foil to keep them warm before serving them all at once.)

PANINI WITH GRILLED ZUCCHINI, RICOTTA SALATA, AND BASIL

Serves 2

Some say it is hard to keep up with the number of zucchini each plant produces, but I don't have that problem. Italians have devised hundreds of ways to cook zucchini, and I've contributed my share.

I enjoy zucchini raw, sliced "carpaccio" style; in pasta sauces; as a vegetable accompaniment to many dishes; and the list goes on.

Grilling zucchini imparts a slightly smoky taste to the sweetness of the vegetable. You can use an outdoor grill, stove-top grill, or the broiler.

> 4 small zucchini
> 3 tablespoons extra virgin olive oil
> 4 slices rustic bread
> Ricotta salata
> Small handful of fresh basil leaves

LIGHT an outdoor or stove-top grill or heat the broiler.

TRIM the stems from the zucchini. Slice lengthwise, about ¼ inch thick.

PLACE the olive oil on a plate and lightly coat each slice of zucchini on both sides. Do not salt, which leaches out juices. Grill the zucchini slices on both sides until tender and slightly browned.

LAY the zucchini over 2 slices of bread. Cover with shavings of ricotta salata. Tear the basil into fragments and sprinkle over the cheese.

TOP with the remaining 2 slices of bread. Press down gently with the palm of your hand to bind the ingredients. Serve immediately.

SUN-DRIED TOMATOES

Principe Borghese tomatoes, which are a medium-size heirloom variety that I grow, are particularly suited to drying. Otherwise, use a fleshy cherry tomato such as the wonderful deep yellow Sungold, a prolific producer of very sweet fruit. The number of tomatoes you dry will depend on your garden yield. Therefore, amounts given are not specific and can be adapted to what is in your garden basket.

Italians use sun-dried tomatoes more as an antipasto than as an ingredient in pastas, risottos, or salads. See page 140 for an antipasto recipe featuring sun-dried tomatoes.

Principe Borghese or other medium vine-ripened tomatoes
Home-dried Italian oregano (page 64)
Whole peeled garlic cloves
Extra virgin olive oil

PLACE the whole tomatoes on a baking sheet, leaving space between them so the warmth can circulate. Turn the oven to the lowest possible setting. Place the tomatoes in the oven and let them dry slowly for 7 hours or longer.

WHEN the tomatoes have shed their excess moisture, but before they become too dry or leathery, remove them from the oven and let cool.

LAYER the tomatoes in a Mason jar with sprinklings of oregano and garlic cloves. Cover with olive oil. Close the jar tightly and keep in the pantry. These tomatoes will keep for months. Just make sure the tomatoes are generously covered in the olive oil, which acts as a preservative by preventing exposure to air. Alternatively, refrigerate the tomatoes in olive oil.

Home-dried Italian Oregano

Italian oregano has an earthy but perfumed quality, less harsh than other varieties. Dried oregano is used more commonly in Italy than fresh. It is one of the few herbs that intensifies in flavor when dry. It is called for in numerous recipes. If I'm using dried oregano in a recipe, I often hold a dried bouquet over the dish and simply shake some of the leaves into the mixture. Also, you will find that some of the leaves will have fallen to the bottom of the bag, and you can reach down and grab a pinch.

To dry oregano, start in the morning just before the oregano is about to bloom. Use garden clippers to cut each mass at the base of the stem. Spread the oregano branches on newspaper, leaving space between the branches and let the surface moisture dry. Gather the oregano branches into "bouquets" about 1 inch thick at the stem ends and tie with twine.

Using twine to create a "clothesline," hang each bouquet stem side up from the twine. Make sure to leave several inches of space between each bunch to allow air to circulate and let dry until the leaves turn from green to gray-green and feel dry to the touch. Time will depend on the temperature indoors.

When the oregano leaves and branches are completely dry, remove them from the clothesline. Place each bouquet in a brown paper bag and close tightly with twine or rubber bands. Store the oregano in a dark, dry place such as a pantry or closet. Use each bouquet one at a time, as needed.

CANDY-SWEET CHOPPED FRESH TOMATOES

Makes 1 cup

When the garden is generous with tomatoes, I cook them in any and all ways. Although this recipe may seem odd, remember that tomatoes are a fruit. It seems only natural to create a marmalade-like condiment. The marmalade tastes delicious spread on morning toast but is also an unusual topping for goat cheese crostini.

4 medium firm red tomatoes
1 heaping tablespoon sugar
1-inch piece vanilla bean, split lengthwise

CUT the tomatoes into small chunks and place them in a large sauté pan. Sprinkle the sugar evenly over the tomatoes and embed the vanilla bean amid the tomato chunks.

TURN the heat to low and cook, stirring, until the sugar melts and tomato juices have evaporated. The tomatoes should be translucent with a bit of syrup remaining in the saucepan. Transfer to a glass jar. Let cool. Cover with a tight-fitting lid and refrigerate.

SALT-CURED NASTURTIUM BUDS

If you have the good fortune of living in a truly Mediterranean climate near the sea, where caper plants grow in the wild and the flower sweetly perfumes the air, you can salt-cure your own capers.

For those of us who can grow delightfully carefree and pretty nasturtiums, adaptable to many climates, a great alternative is making salt-cured nasturtium buds, remarkably satisfactory as a substitute. Don't forget that both the flower and leaves of nasturtiums are edible and can be used in salads, in antipasti, and as edible garnishes.

Pick the buds when they are about the size of small capers.

Nasturtium buds, as many as you can gather
Coarse sea salt, as much as needed
Black peppercorns, a few for flavoring

WIPE the nasturtium buds clean with a kitchen towel, rubbing the surface gently to make sure they are free of grit and soil.

PLACE the buds in a glass jar. Cover them completely in coarse salt. Let rest for 2 to 3 hours.

REMOVE the nasturtium buds from the salt and wipe them free of salt and moisture. Place them along with a few peppercorns in a glass jar with a tight-fitting lid and store in the pantry.

ROSE-SCENTED CUSTARD

Serves 4

Summer and roses are a heady combination. This innocent-looking dessert will transport you to a rose garden in full bloom. Be sure to use roses that have not been sprayed.

3 large egg yolks

1½ cups whipping cream

⅓ cup sugar, plus extra for sprinkling

1 teaspoon vanilla extract

3 tablespoons rose water

Small roses or rose petals

BUTTER four ½-cup custard cups and set aside. Preheat the oven to 325°F and bring a kettle of water to a boil.

PLACE the egg yolks in a bowl and whisk lightly. Combine the cream and sugar in a small saucepan and heat just long enough to dissolve the sugar. Let cool completely and pour into the bowl containing the egg yolks, whisking as you add the cream. Add the vanilla and rose water and stir.

POUR the custard mixture into the custard cups. Arrange the custard cups in the pan. Fill with enough boiling water to come a third of the way up the sides of the custard cups.

BAKE for 15 to 20 minutes, or until just set. Carefully remove the custard cups from the water bath.

SET the oven on broil. Sprinkle a little sugar over the tops of the custards. Place them under the broiler for just a minute to brown the tops. Garnish with fragrant small roses or rose petals. Serve tepid or cold.

MY RICOTTA DESSERT

Serves 4 to 5

This poetic dessert requires no cooking, a bonus during warm weather. With a dollop of glossy Meyer lemon marmalade as a topping and a garnish of jasmine blossoms, this sweet ricotta will delight all your senses.

> One 15-ounce container whole-milk ricotta
> 1/4 cup sugar
> 1/3 cup almonds, toasted (page 29) and chopped
> 2 tablespoons chopped bittersweet chocolate
> Almond oil
> Meyer Lemon Marmellata (page 238)
> Jasmine flowers for garnish, if available

With a bowl underneath to catch the liquid, **PLACE** the ricotta in a colander lined with cheesecloth. Tie the ends of the cheesecloth together and place a weight on top. Refrigerate and let drain for at least 1 hour or overnight.

WHISK the ricotta until smooth and fluffy. Stir in the sugar, almonds, and chocolate until evenly incorporated.

USE almond oil to lightly coat 4 or 5 custard cups. Pack the ricotta mixture into the cups. Cover with wax paper and refrigerate to firm up the ricotta.

To serve, gently **UNMOLD** onto individual dessert dishes. Top each serving with a spoonful of the lemon marmalade. Garnish with small sprays of jasmine.

MEYER LEMON GELATO TOPPED WITH FRESH FIGS AND PISTACHIOS

Makes 1 pint

It is a thrill to have a generous crop of Meyer lemons. I use not only the juice in many recipes but also the fragrant peel. This gelato is infused with a generous amount of fresh-picked lemon peel. Garnished with figs and pistachios, it is a beautiful sight to behold, and the flavors and textures combine to create a very special gelato dessert. Substitute organic Eureka lemons if Meyer lemons are unavailable.

> 2 cups whole milk
> $^1/_2$ cup sugar
> Yellow peel of 2 large Meyer lemons, in long, wide ribbonlike strands
>   (use a vegetable peeler)
> 4 large egg yolks
> 3 or 4 fresh figs, sliced
> Chopped pistachios

PLACE the milk, ¼ cup of the sugar, and the lemon peel in a saucepan and bring to a boil. Remove from heat. Cover and set aside until the milk is strongly perfumed with lemon, about 30 minutes or up to an hour. Check occasionally until the lemon presence is strong but not overpowering. Remember that when frozen, the flavor will lose some of its intensity.

In a medium bowl, **WHISK** together the remaining ¼ cup sugar and the egg yolks until the mixture thickens and turns pale yellow.

STRAIN the milk mixture into a medium bowl to remove the lemon peel, letting as much milk as possible drain from the peel. Measure the milk and add more if needed to make 2 cups.

(continued)

PLACE the milk in a saucepan and bring to a boil. Remove from the heat and slowly whisk half the milk into the egg and sugar mixture. Whisk in the remaining milk.

POUR the milk-egg mixture back into the saucepan and place over medium heat. Using a wooden spoon, stir constantly until the mixture is thick enough to coat the back of the spoon. Pour into a bowl and keep stirring until the mixture cools.

FREEZE in an ice-cream machine following the manufacturer's directions.

To serve, **SCOOP** the gelato into chilled metal or glass goblets. Garnish with fresh fig slices and chopped pistachios.

MINT GELATO TOPPED WITH SHAVINGS OF DARKEST CHOCOLATE

Makes 1 pint

Mint ice cream has been a favorite of mine since I was a little girl, back when it was dyed green. I always ordered the mint ice cream with chocolate flecks in it. Now that I am all grown up, I like my mint ice cream to taste like mint but be creamy white. Wandering through the garden, I love it when, without realizing, I step on some mint and its fragrance rises up to my nose. Since mint grows here and there all over the garden, this happens on a somewhat regular basis. In this recipe, mint infuses the custard base with its special candy-sweet fragrance. Instead of incorporating frozen-solid bits of chocolate within the gelato, I prefer to shave darkest chocolate over the top.

> 2 cups whole milk
> 1/2 cup sugar
> 1 cup torn mint leaves
> 4 large egg yolks
> Dark chocolate

PLACE the milk, 1/4 cup of the sugar, and the mint in a saucepan and bring to a boil. Remove from heat. Cover and set aside until the milk is strongly perfumed with mint, about 30 minutes or up to an hour. Check occasionally until the mint presence is strong but not overpowering. Remember that when frozen, the flavor will lose some of its intensity.

In a small bowl, **WHISK** together the remaining 1/4 cup sugar and the egg yolks until the mixture thickens and turns pale yellow.

STRAIN the milk mixture into a medium bowl to remove the mint leaves, letting as much milk as possible drain from the leaves. Measure the milk and add more if needed to make 2 cups.

(continued)

PLACE the milk in a saucepan and bring to a boil. Remove from the heat and slowly whisk half the milk into the egg and sugar mixture. Whisk in the remaining milk.

POUR the milk-egg mixture back into the saucepan and place over medium heat. Using a wooden spoon, stir constantly until the mixture is thick enough to coat the back of the spoon. Pour into a bowl and keep stirring until the mixture cools.

FREEZE in an ice-cream machine following the manufacturer's directions.

To serve, **SCOOP** the gelato into chilled metal or glass goblets. Shave the chocolate over the top.

MEYER LEMON GRANITA

Serves 6

Lemon granita is a summertime staple in Italy, eaten morning, noon, and night. My mother told me that *granita di limone* with brioche was eaten on those Palermo mornings when it was too hot to have the usual caffè latte.

If Meyer lemons are unavailable, substitute organic market lemons and increase the sugar to about $^3/_4$ cup.

    $^1/_2$ cup sugar
    1 cup freshly squeezed Meyer lemon juice, strained of seeds and pulp
    Lemon blossoms and leaves, if available

STIR together 1 cup water and the sugar until the sugar dissolves. Add another 2 cups water and the lemon juice. Stir well. Transfer the mixture to a pie tin and place in the freezer.

After about 30 minutes, ice crystals will begin to form. **STIR** the mixture well, breaking up the ice crystals. Return it to the freezer and continue to break up the crystals at 30-minute intervals. The finished product will be slushy, with small icy granules.

If not serving immediately, **TRANSFER** the granita to a glass or plastic container with a tightly fitting lid.

SERVE in chilled glass or metal ice-cream goblets. Garnish with a few blossoms if you can spare them. Or simply place a fragrant lemon leaf atop each serving.

FALL

SAN FRANCISCO'S TRADITIONAL WARM season is fall—a brief Indian summer. My hollyhocks still blossom pink, maroon, and white—ruffled crepe-paper petals on absurdly tall spires. They are always a delight to me. The few blossoms on my struggling bougainvillea, its tiny white dot centering each magenta star-shaped flower, are beginning to fade, but they still evoke the Mediterranean to me. They look especially at home against the tall wall. The emerald green mosses that grow so velvety in cool weather turn brown during our summer (mildly hot by most standards).

With autumn comes the occasional heat wave. The moss dries up completely and simply turns ashen, falling away to fully reveal the wall—the swirling rivers of stone, the mineral tones of ocher, bone-white, rust, and violet, the colors of a fresco from antiquity.

The artichokes are vigorous now. They grow magnificently well here—sea air, temperate climate. Bigger and bigger they grow, with silvery serrated leaves longer than four feet at the base, and coarse to the touch. The new growth is light gray and downy. Even if it didn't bear artichokes, this plant would impress with its sublime silver-green color and large fountainlike growing habit.

Books say to plant artichokes six to eight feet apart, but my neighbors Ginetta and Giovanni plant them much more closely, which seems to help support the heavier, larger leaves. My plants come from their thinning, tossed over the fence into my waiting hands.

Four plants grow in a line next to my late-fruiting San Piero fig tree. A few of the fig tree's leaves are only now beginning to curl up and turn brown and crinkly. Otherwise, it is still leafy with its distinctive three-lobed green leaves, big as a giant's hand. As the tree grows taller, it will provide a very pleasant shady spot to sit or lounge.

Next spring, I'll plant an Adriatic fig, a green-skinned variety with that breathtaking violet flesh dripping with honey. I now know it is the best for coastal growing. Ginetta and Giovanni already know this. Their fig tree, a large Adriatic, bears fruit early. In fall, its leafless structure is striking against the sunniest wall in the garden.

My olive trees, the Leccino variety, were once mere saplings. They have grown rapidly and produced fruit. The precious green olives are turning to russet. After the *raccolta*, the harvest, the leaves will remain year-round to shimmer and shine in the dark winter months ahead.

At the end of summer I cut down the oregano branches at their base. I dried the leafy stalks and stored them in the dark pantry in brown paper bags. I use the dried oregano in many dishes. I even save the stems. I arrange them, still tied in twine, in a long, narrow glass vase in the *sala d'ingresso*, or foyer, of my home, as a reminder of summer. When I walk by, I give the twigs a loving look. But already fresh oregano has grown back abundantly. In the warmth of Indian summer, the fall herb garden is redolent of rosemary, sage, winter savory—the most strongly scented herbs of summer.

Sage is not an herb I used much in the past. However, the garden has worked its magic and now it has become a favorite of mine. I toss it into simple soups, pasta sauces, vegetable tortas. The woodsy scent and feltlike gray-green leaves give dishes a tonic flavor and aroma. Its natural antibiotic properties aren't lost on me when I have a bout of influenza or feel run-down and vulnerable.

Two Meyer lemon trees dangle green fruits. They entice me with the golden harvest to come. Winter won't interrupt the cycle of fruits and blossoms. The evergreen leaves alone are intensely fragrant. When passing by a tree, I'll often pluck a leaf and tear it in half to breathe in its lemony perfume. I use the leaves to flavor dishes.

My mother often spoke about the huge park outside Palermo where large tracts of citronella trees grew. So, I am training my citronella—lemon verbena—to be a tree instead of a bush, trimming out branches to promote upward growth. The green leaves, strongly citrus-scented, are narrow and pointed, and tiny mauve blossoms grow in delicate sprays from the newest of leaves.

Chives grow, and there are many blossoms to deadhead. I leave some of the spent ones on the plant since I like their autumnal shade of sun-bleached gray-lavender. I touch the petals and they feel papery-dry.

This fall, I've made a dramatic decision. I plan to relocate the hydrangeas. They were given to me by a neighbor whose hydrangea garden was becoming overcrowded. The plants were mature when they went into the ground. They run the full length of the west wall. The sturdy shrubs do offer big, blowsy blooms from spring into fall. I'll group them together in the only remaining shady corner of the garden.

The first season, though, I was thrilled with the sinuous ribbon of shell-pink to carnelian pom-poms. In their place, pretty as they might be, I want more of the dry-landscape plants of the south of Italy so meaningful to me—oleanders, pittosporum, tamarisk trees, a loquat tree. I'll plant a pomegranate and hope it will bear fruit, or at least pretty orange flowers. I've already replaced two hydrangeas with the chaste white petals of Sister Agnes oleanders.

I make a final effort to weed out the oxalis, every gardener's nightmare. It is the only weed I truly consider unwelcome. It is aggressive and relentlessly, unbearably invasive. I turn over the soil to aerate it in anticipation of winter. I do a general sweeping and tidying up of the large paved back terrace. I pull out the tomato plants that are now just spindly and spidery brown branches shrouded in masses of dead leaves.

Looking over the garden, I find many things to delight my eyes—the shiny palm, the tall cypresses, the chicories, the herbs that continue to thrive. Nasturtiums still trail cream, cherry, and orange blossoms from one terrace down to the next. The fall garden is splendid, slowly transforming from bright to muted as Indian summer ends and woodsmoke scents the cool days ahead.

ANTIPASTI · *Starters*

Adriatic Figs Stuffed with Stracchino Cheese   81

Autumn Antipasto Basket   82

Bresaola Involtini   84

Whole Sage Leaves in Pastella   85

Warm Crostini Topped with Dolcelatte Gorgonzola Butter   87

INSALATE · *Salads*

Fall Caprese   88

Giovanni's Pan di Zucchero Salad   89

Radicchio di Castelfranco with Toasted Almonds and Warm Butter   91

Salad of Radicchio Leaves and Nasturtiums with New-Crop Walnuts   92

Chioggia Beet and Radicchio Salad   93

Insalata di Rinforzo   95

MINESTRE · *Soups*

Vegetable Broth with Fennel, Herbs, and Dried Parmesan Cheese Rind   97

Lacinato Kale Soup with Rosemary-scented Rustic Bread Cubes   98

Assorted Green Chicory Soup with Borlotti Beans and Pancetta   100

PASTA

Spaghetti with Romanesco Broccoli and Black Olives   101

Orecchiette with Cima di Rapa and Hot Red Pepper   103

Pasta with Young Artichokes, Parsley, and White Wine   104

Fettuccine with Sautéed Radicchio, Grappa-soaked Raisins, and Truffle Oil   105

RISOTTO

Risotto with Green Tomatoes   106

Risotto with Pink Radicchio and Golden Beets   108

Artichoke and Leek Risotto with Cream   110

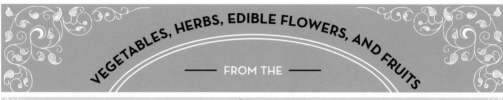

· Fall Garden ·

Alloro · European bay

Basilico Genovese · Genoa basil

Bieta verde · Swiss chard

Bietola di Chioggia · Chioggia beets

Carota rossa · red carrots

Cicoria Pan di Zucchero · pale green chicory

Cicoria rossa di Treviso · Treviso radicchio

Cicoria variegato di Castelfranco · variegated cream and pink Castelfranco radicchio

Cima di rapa · broccoli rabe

Erbette · cut-and-come-again ribless chard

Fagioli rampicante lingua di fuoco · climbing borlotti beans

Finocchio · bulb fennel

Golden beets

Indivia riccia · curly endive

Kumquats

Lacinato (Tuscan) kale

Maggiorana gentile · sweet marjoram

Nasturzio · nasturtium leaves, flowers, and buds

Origano · Italian oregano

Pomodori verdi · green tomatoes

Prezzemolo comune · small flat-leaf Italian parsley

Prezzemolo gigante di Napoli · large flat-leaf Neapolitan parsley

Principe Borghese tomatoes

Rapa bianca · white turnip

Romanesco broccoli · green cauliflower

Rosmarino · rosemary

Rucola selvatica · wild arugula

Salvia officinale · sage

San Piero figs

Satureja montana · winter savory

Timo · thyme

ADRIATIC FIGS STUFFED WITH STRACCHINO CHEESE

Serves 4

With their pale green skin and brilliant pink-violet flesh, Adriatic figs are easily one of my favorite fruits. Their extraordinary honeyed flavor ensures a sublime eating experience. Warming the figs gently brings out the perfume of the fruit. A dollop of creamy Stracchino cheese and a drizzling of intense honey could be called gilding the lily, but it truly ends up a superb combination of flavors.

> 8 large Adriatic figs or other variety of fresh fig
> 8 ounces (about 1 cup) Stracchino cheese or ricotta, at room temperature
> Honey, at pourable temperature
> Coarsely ground black pepper

PREHEAT the oven to 325°F.

TRIM the stems and cut the figs in half horizontally. Arrange in a baking dish cut side up and place in the oven until just warmed through, about 5 minutes.

TRANSFER the figs to a serving platter. Place a tablespoon of Stracchino at the center of each fig half. Drizzle with honey and sprinkle with pepper. Serve immediately.

AUTUMN ANTIPASTO BASKET

This leisurely and communal beginning to a meal promotes conversation and camaraderie. And nothing could look fresher or be simpler to assemble than this glorious expression of the fall season. Arrange the offering in a lovely rustic basket lined with a coarse linen napkin like those oversized ones used in Italy, or simply use a woven cotton white napkin.

    Assorted young pink and red radicchio leaves
    White chicory leaves, such as Pan di Zucchero chicory, or tender
        inner leaves of escarole
    Bunch of crisp grapes
    New-crop walnuts in the shell
    Extra virgin olive oil
    Sea salt

WASH the radicchio and chicory leaves and allow to dry on a clean dishtowel. Use kitchen shears to cut the grapes into small clusters.

LINE a basket with a large napkin. Arrange the radicchio and chicory leaves in the basket and nestle the grape clusters and walnuts among the leaves.

POUR olive oil into a small shallow bowl. Place a small saucer of sea salt, a nut-cracker, and the olive oil on the dining table. Set the basket next to the condiments.

Each person **DIPS** the radicchio or chicory leaves into the olive oil and sprinkles the leaves with salt. The nuts are cracked open and the nut meats extracted. The grapes are plucked off the clusters one by one. Each guest should alternate the different offerings in the basket, perhaps first eating a pungent chicory leaf, then a sweet grape, then a walnut.

BRESAOLA INVOLTINI

Makes 6 involtini

Rughetta is the Italian name for wild arugula. It has smaller leaves than its cultivated counterpart, with sharply serrated edges, and is crisp and succulent.

Bresaola, cured beef filet or loin, is purchased sliced to order and must be eaten as soon as possible or it will dry out. Here, it is wrapped around peppery sprigs of wild arugula to form the involtini, or stuffed rolls.

Prepare the involtini just before serving. Guests can use a knife and fork or eat with their fingers if part of a picnic lunch.

Handful of wild or cultivated arugula sprigs, plus extra for garnish,
    stems trimmed
Extra virgin olive oil
Lemon juice
Sea salt
6 slices bresaola
6 lemon wedges

PLACE the arugula sprigs in a bowl. Season with olive oil, lemon juice, and salt to taste.

Carefully PLACE individual bresaola slices on a work surface. Put a few sprigs of the dressed arugula on one side of each slice of bresaola. Gently roll the bresaola around the greens until the bresaola folds over itself.

PLACE the involtini on a serving platter. Drizzle lightly with olive oil. Garnish with arugula sprigs and lemon wedges.

WHOLE SAGE LEAVES IN PASTELLA

Serves 4

A *pastella* is the classic Italian batter for deep-frying or shallow-frying vegetables. In contact with hot olive oil, the pastella's protective layer forms a thin, crisp coating that seals in flavor and juices and adds a nice bit of crunch. Large sage leaves, just picked to ensure tenderness, respond beautifully to this treatment.

Serve the sage fritters on their own as a light antipasto before dinner, along with a glass of crisp, cold white wine to whet the appetite for the meal that follows.

16 large sage leaves
^{2}/$_3$ cup unbleached all-purpose flour
Extra virgin olive oil
Sea salt

PREHEAT the oven to 200°F.

USE a damp clean dishtowel to wipe the sage leaves clean. Set the leaves on a dry dishtowel and let them air-dry.

PLACE the flour in a small bowl. Slowly beat in about 1 cup water with a fork or whisk, or enough until the batter attains the texture of thick cream.

ADD enough olive oil to a sauté pan to come ½ inch up the side of the pan. When the oil is hot but not smoking, dip 3 or 4 sage leaves at a time in the batter and let the excess batter drip off. Carefully slip the leaves into the hot oil and fry until the crust is golden, turning once to fry the other side, a total of 3 or 4 minutes. Carefully remove the leaves from the oil without breaking the crust. A slotted metal spatula works well and allows excess oil to drain back into the pan. (continued)

PLACE the leaves on paper towels to absorb excess oil. Sprinkle with salt while hot. Keep warm on a platter in a warm oven.

REPEAT the procedure with the remaining leaves.

ARRANGE 4 leaves on each of 4 small plates and serve immediately while hot and crisp.

WARM CROSTINI TOPPED WITH DOLCELATTE GORGONZOLA BUTTER

Serves 4

Treviso radicchio is particularly succulent when raw, with a more tender leaf and juicy rib than the more common round radicchio. Finely chopped radicchio and walnuts sprinkled over Gorgonzola butter add a pleasing bitter vegetable flavor that contrasts well with the rich, creamy spread.

> 1 small baguette, cut into 12 thin rounds
>
> 3 tablespoons unsalted butter, at room temperature
>
> 3 tablespoons Dolcelatte Gorgonzola cheese, at room temperature
>
> 1 small Treviso or round red radicchio, cored and finely chopped, a few whole leaves
> reserved for garnish
>
> Handful of freshly cracked walnut meats, lightly toasted (see page 93) and finely
> chopped

PREHEAT the oven to 375°F.

ARRANGE the bread rounds on a baking sheet. Bake for approximately 3 minutes, or until light golden. Remove the sheet from the oven and turn the crostini to lightly brown the other side. Remove from the oven and set aside.

PLACE the butter and Gorgonzola in a small bowl and mash together until thoroughly blended. Spread each crostini with the Gorgonzola mixture and sprinkle with chopped radicchio and walnuts. Arrange on a platter. Garnish with radicchio leaves.

FALL CAPRESE

Serves 4

Here is my autumn version of caprese. Make sure the olives are crisp and the flesh is evenly green throughout. If new-crop walnuts are available, use them. They arrive at the very beginning of the season when the shells have just hardened and the walnut meat is milky-white and crisp. Otherwise, lightly toast shelled walnuts and let cool before coarsely chopping them.

Four 4-ounce fresh mozzarella balls, brought to room temperature
16 crisp green olives such as the large Baresane variety
12 new-crop walnuts in the shell, shelled and coarsely chopped
6 to 8 tablespoons extra virgin olive oil
Zest of $\frac{1}{2}$ small lemon
2 tablespoons coarsely chopped fresh flat-leaf parsley
Sea salt
Freshly ground black pepper

SLICE the mozzarella into rounds. If very moist, drain on a kitchen towel.

USE a paring knife to cut thick strips of olive flesh from the pits. Coarsely chop the olives.

ARRANGE the mozzarella on a serving platter. Sprinkle the olives over the mozzarella rounds. Sprinkle the walnuts over the olives. Drizzle with olive oil. Sprinkle the lemon zest and parsley over the cheese, and season with salt and pepper to taste. Serve immediately.

GIOVANNI'S PAN DI ZUCCHERO SALAD

Serves 2

My neighbors Giovanni and Ginetta are one of the last of the Italian families left in my neighborhood, once predominantly Italian many years ago. Almost on a daily basis, except on the coldest or rainiest days, Giovanni makes a trip up and down his garden's length and, using an old-fashioned hose with a wide spray nozzle, checks each plant and determines whether or not it's thirsty and needs a drink of water.

I'm a big proponent of this method of watering. Yes, it is time-consuming. But each plant has differing needs, and even within the same batch of, say, parsley, one side may be more dried out than another. It also creates an important communion between the plant and the gardener. It gives me time to study each one, meditate for a few moments, and in this way, anticipate the plant's needs or detect a problem early on, before it becomes too late. This is one of the secrets of being a successful gardener—looking carefully and regularly at each plant.

Giovanni and Ginetta routinely toss over the fence a wonderful bag of greens or hand over a basket of their big bumpy lemons (not citrons), a variety I see around San Francisco in old gardens. One day, a plump oval of tightly furled palest green leaves was tossed to me over the fence. "Pan di Zucchero," Giovanni said. "Cut it into slivers, add some thinly sliced onions, and olive oil, red wine vinegar, and salt." I went directly up to the kitchen and made the salad. Now I have Pan di Zucchero chicory, which means sugared or sweet bread in Italian, in my garden. It is one of my favorite chicories. The name refers to the tender silky leaves, which are less bitter than most chicories, and to its loaf-of-bread shape.

1 small head Pan di Zucchero chicory or tender inner leaves of escarole

1/2 small onion, sliced and soaked in several changes of water to remove its "bite"

Extra virgin olive oil

Best-quality red wine vinegar

Sea salt

REMOVE any damaged outer leaves from the chicory and rinse well. Finely slice the "loaf" of chicory crosswise.

DRAIN the onion and pat dry.

PLACE the chicory and onion in a shallow salad bowl. Drizzle with a generous amount of olive oil and vinegar, and season with salt to taste. Serve immediately.

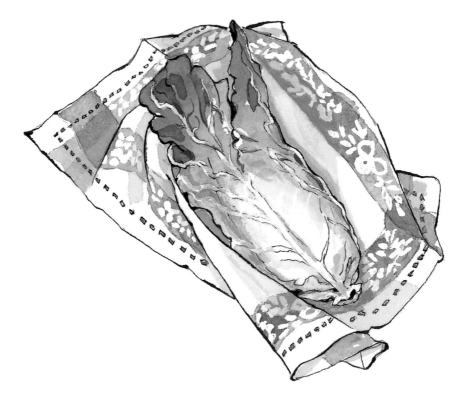

RADICCHIO DI CASTELFRANCO WITH TOASTED ALMONDS AND WARM BUTTER

Serves 4

Perhaps the most spectacular radicchio of all is the variegated one from Castelfranco. Its pale green leaves flecked with pink and rose make it special. But this particular radicchio also boasts very tender leaves, making it an ideal salad ingredient.

Combined with almonds and warm butter, and topped with shavings of Parmigiano-Reggiano, the salad is extremely sophisticated and appropriate for the most festive of occasions.

> 1 head variegated radicchio di Castelfranco or round red radicchio
> 1/4 cup slivered almonds, lightly toasted (see page 29)
> 2 tablespoons unsalted butter
> 2 tablespoons extra virgin olive oil
> Sea salt
> Parmigiano-Reggiano cheese

CORE the radicchio and tear into bite-size pieces. Place on a large serving platter and toss with the almonds.

MELT the butter over low heat. Pour over the salad and toss. Drizzle with olive oil and add salt to taste. Toss again. Just before serving, use a vegetable peeler to cover the salad with paper-thin shavings of Parmesan, and give the salad one last toss.

SALAD OF RADICCHIO LEAVES AND NASTURTIUMS WITH NEW-CROP WALNUTS

Serves 4

Although this salad seems to exist merely to be decorative, nothing could be further from the truth. The tonic radicchio leaves, the amazing nutritional properties found in edible flowers, and the healthfulness of walnuts make this extraordinarily pretty traditional rustic Italian salad a dish of real substance. Use the round red radicchio.

4 cups torn radicchio leaves
$^1/_3$ cup walnuts, toasted (see page 93) and coarsely chopped
3 tablespoons extra virgin olive oil
Sea salt
Parmigiano-Reggiano cheese
Handful of nasturtium blossoms in assorted colors

In a large shallow serving bowl, **TOSS** the radicchio and walnuts. Drizzle with olive oil and sprinkle with salt to taste; toss again until the leaves are glossy.

Just before serving, **USE** a vegetable peeler to shave Parmesan over the salad; sprinkle with nasturtium blossoms.

CHIOGGIA BEET AND RADICCHIO SALAD

Serves 4

With its candylike swirled markings of pink and white flesh, the Chioggia beet could not be lovelier. Its sweet flavor tastes almost like candy, but with an earthy quality.

For this salad I've paired the beets with tart radicchio, walnuts, and (surprise!) diced candied citron to echo the sweetness of the beets. The citron also lends its yellow-green translucent sparkle.

> **6 Chioggia or other small to medium beets with greens still attached**
> **Sea salt**
> **Handful of new-crop walnuts in the shell**
> **1 medium or 2 small heads Treviso or round red radicchio**
> **Extra virgin olive oil**
> **¼ cup finely diced candied citron**

TRIM the beet tops, leaving just the base of the leaves attached to the root. (Save the greens for a quick sauté or soup.) Place the beets in a bowl of tepid water and agitate them to help dislodge soil.

FILL a medium saucepan with enough salted water to generously cover the beets and bring to a boil. Immerse the beets and cook for 10 to 20 minutes, depending on size. Use a thin, long wooden skewer to test one beet for doneness. When the skewer penetrates the beet with a touch of resistance, drain the beets. Peel when cool enough to handle, being careful not to get the beet juice on your clothing. Cut into medium dice.

While the beets are cooling, **PREHEAT** the oven to 350°F. Crack the walnuts and remove any tough membranes. Place on a baking sheet and toast until light golden, about 8 minutes. Shake the baking sheet occasionally to distribute the heat. Remove the walnuts from the oven. Let cool and coarsely chop. *(continued)*

REMOVE any bruised outer leaves from the radicchio. Core and slice crosswise into medium-thin slivers.

PLACE the beets, radicchio, and walnuts in a shallow serving dish and gently toss. Drizzle with olive oil until lightly coated. Add salt to taste. Sprinkle the citron over the top.

INSALATA DI RINFORZO

Serves 4

The classic version of this salad is served in Italy when the weather starts to turn cool. It takes advantage of all the root vegetables in the garden as well as cold-hardy cauliflower. Although white cauliflower is normally used, I have used my chartreuse Romanesco broccoli, which is in fact a cauliflower, picked from my vegetable patch. With its oddly shaped conical peaks, it is an unusually handsome vegetable that is exceedingly tender and sweet. It turns a traditional dish into a decidedly nontraditional one.

I've simply added brilliantly colored red carrots preserved in red wine vinegar to the green cauliflower, tangy olives, and salt-cured nasturtium buds. This salad is striking to look at, as well as a piquant wake-up call to the appetite.

2 heads Romanesco broccoli, white cauliflower, or Broccoflower,
    leaves cut away, core trimmed
Sea salt
$1/4$ cup extra virgin olive oil
$1/4$ cup best-quality white wine vinegar
$1/2$ cup finely diced Red Carrots sott'Aceto (page 183)
$1/2$ cup pitted oil-cured black olives, coarsely chopped
$1/4$ cup Salt-cured Nasturtium Buds (page 66) or salt-cured capers,
    salt wiped off with a paper towel
$1/2$ cup coarsely chopped fresh flat-leaf parsley

PLUNGE the whole cauliflowers into a large pot of boiling salted water. Cook until al dente, about 10 minutes. Drain and set aside to cool. Carefully core the cauliflowers, cut into bite-size florets, and place in a shallow serving bowl. *(continued)*

ADD the olive oil and vinegar and very gently toss. Add the carrots, olives, nasturtium buds, and parsley. Toss gently and set aside for an hour at room temperature for flavors to mellow.

VEGETABLE BROTH WITH FENNEL, HERBS, AND DRIED PARMESAN CHEESE RIND

Makes approximately 1½ quarts

Fresh fennel from the fall garden imparts a surprising sweetness to the broth. Use this as a base for soups and risottos. On its own, this broth makes a wonderful tonic to sip any time of the day.

> 2 tablespoons extra virgin olive oil
> 4 garlic cloves, coarsely chopped
> 3 carrots, sliced
> 2 leeks, root ends and half of green tops trimmed, sliced
> 1 fennel bulb, thickly sliced
> 2 celery stalks, sliced, and leaves chopped
> 2 Principe Borghese or other medium vine-ripened tomatoes, diced
> 3 sprigs fresh flat-leaf parsley
> 3 sprigs fresh basil
> 2 fresh bay leaves
> 12 black peppercorns
> Dried Parmesan cheese rind (about ¼ cup of pieces)
> Sea salt

HEAT the olive oil in a soup pot, add the garlic, and sauté over very low heat for several minutes. Add the carrots, leeks, fennel, and celery and sauté briefly. Add the tomatoes, parsley, basil, bay leaves, and peppercorns and sauté for a couple of minutes.

ADD 7 cups water and the Parmesan rind. Cover and bring to a boil. Lower the heat and simmer, partly covered, for about 1 hour, adding salt to taste toward the end of the cooking time. Strain. Use immediately or refrigerate for up to 2 days.

LACINATO KALE SOUP WITH ROSEMARY-SCENTED RUSTIC BREAD CUBES

Serves 4

Lacinato kale, also known as Tuscan or black kale, looks very different from ordinary kale. It has a very long narrow leaf, crinkly surface, and very dark green color. It is a good producer in my cool climate. Here the flavor of kale is enlivened with assertive rosemary and hot red pepper.

FOR THE SOUP

3 tablespoons extra virgin olive oil, plus extra for drizzling

1/8 teaspoon hot red pepper flakes, or to taste

1 garlic clove, coarsely chopped

1/2 medium onion, finely diced

1 pound lacinato kale (the younger the better), stemmed and cut crosswise into thick ribbons

Sea salt

FOR THE BREAD CUBES

3 tablespoons unsalted butter

2 teaspoons finely chopped fresh rosemary

1 1/2 cups 3/4-inch rustic bread cubes

1 garlic clove, finely chopped

TO FINISH

Shaved pecorino cheese

PLACE the olive oil, red pepper, garlic, and onion in a soup pot. Cook over very low heat until the onion softens, about 5 minutes, stirring often.

ADD the kale and salt to taste, and stir with a wooden spoon until the kale wilts slightly. Add 4 cups water. Bring to a boil; then lower the heat to a simmer. Cook until the kale is tender, about 10 minutes.

Meanwhile, **PLACE** the butter and rosemary in a large sauté pan. Warm over low heat until the rosemary releases its perfume. Add the bread, raise the heat to medium, and stir the bread cubes until they absorb the flavored butter and become golden and crunchy. A minute or so before they are done, lower the heat and sprinkle the garlic over the bread. Toss briefly until the garlic is cooked but before it colors.

When the kale is tender, **LADLE** the soup into individual shallow soup bowls. Top with the bread cubes and stir once. Drizzle a little olive oil over each bowl of soup and top with a few shavings of pecorino.

ASSORTED GREEN CHICORY SOUP WITH BORLOTTI BEANS AND PANCETTA

Serves 4

This soup is a combination of many green chicories that I grow, from delicate pastel yellow Pan di Zucchero to dark green radicchios, also members of the chicory family. As I add a few leaves of each one to my garden basket, the beauty of the varied shapes and colors of leaves makes me feel a sense of wonder at nature's incredible gifts.

3 tablespoons extra virgin olive oil, plus extra for drizzling
1 tablespoon chopped pancetta
$1/2$ medium onion, finely chopped
1 fresh bay leaf, torn in half
2 garlic cloves, lightly crushed
$1/2$ pound assorted chicories, leaves cut into $3/4$-inch ribbons
Sea salt
1 cup cooked borlotti or pinto beans (see page 169)

In a medium soup pot, **PLACE** the olive oil, pancetta, onion, and bay leaf. Sauté over low heat until the onion is soft and translucent, about 8 minutes. Add the garlic and sauté for 3 to 4 minutes.

ADD the chicory and stir with a wooden spoon to flavor the greens. Add 4 cups water and salt to taste. Bring to a boil, then simmer, uncovered, until the greens are tender, 5 to 10 minutes. Toward the end of the cooking time, gently stir in the cooked beans and heat through.

LADLE into shallow bowls and drizzle a little olive oil over the soup.

SPAGHETTI WITH ROMANESCO BROCCOLI AND BLACK OLIVES

Serves 4

In Italy, cauliflower can be white, purple, or light green. The variety I've used here is Romanesco broccoli, but it is actually a green cauliflower. Very delicate in taste and texture, it requires a watchful eye to avoid overcooking. Ricotta salata is fresh ricotta salted to shed moisture. It is tangy and moist, but firm.

6 tablespoons extra virgin olive oil

$1/2$ medium onion, finely diced

2 small heads Romanesco broccoli,
    white cauliflower, or Broccoflower

Sea salt

12 oil-cured black olives, pitted and coarsely chopped

1 pound imported thick or regular spaghetti

Freshly ground black pepper

$1/4$ cup freshly grated pecorino Romano cheese, plus extra
    for serving

Ricotta salata, shaved paper-thin

HEAT the olive oil in a large sauté pan and add the onion. Cook over low heat until soft and translucent, about 8 minutes.

CORE the cauliflowers and cut into bite-size florets. Add the cauliflower, ¾ cup water, and a touch of salt to the onion; cook at a simmer until the florets are tender but hold their shape. Stir in the olives and simmer until hot.

(continued)

Meanwhile, **BRING** a large pot of salted water to a boil and cook the spaghetti until al dente. Drain.

TOSS the pasta with the sauce. Season with pepper to taste. Sprinkle about ¼ cup pecorino over the pasta and gently toss. Top with shavings of ricotta salata. Serve with additional grated pecorino at the table.

ORECCHIETTE WITH CIMA DI RAPA AND HOT RED PEPPER

Serves 4 to 6

One bite of this little ear-shaped pasta tossed with bitter *cima di rapa*, broccoli rabe, transports me to Puglia. Perhaps no other dish is more representative of this region. It is with great satisfaction that I cook this dish with broccoli rabe from my own garden. Puglia, especially the southern tip, has been a major inspiration in choosing what to plant here at home.

>   Sea salt
>   1 pound imported orecchiette
>   1 pound broccoli rabe, thick stems trimmed, coarsely chopped
> $1/2$ cup extra virgin olive oil
>   3 garlic cloves, chopped
>   Hot red pepper flakes
>   4 salt-cured anchovy fillets, salt scraped off with a knife
>   Pinch of home-dried Italian oregano (page 64)
>   Freshly grated pecorino Romano cheese (optional)

BRING a large pot of salted water to a boil. Add the orecchiette and stir. When the water returns to a boil, add the broccoli rabe.

Meanwhile, in a very large sauté pan over low heat, **WARM** the olive oil, garlic, and red pepper. When the garlic colors lightly, add the anchovies. Stir with a wooden spoon until the anchovy pieces melt into the olive oil. Set aside.

When the orecchiette are al dente, **DRAIN** the pasta and greens, leaving them just a little wet. Add them to the sauté pan along with the oregano and toss briefly over high heat for about a minute. Taste and add salt if needed. If desired, sprinkle with pecorino.

PASTA WITH YOUNG ARTICHOKES, PARSLEY, AND WHITE WINE

Serves 4 to 6

Just-picked artichokes retain all the moisture and flavor that the market vegetable tends to lose. You will be amazed at how easily the knife glides through the tender leaves, heart, and stems, and at the intensely mineral flavor of the artichoke.

Sea salt
5 tablespoons extra virgin olive oil
$1/2$ cup chopped fresh flat-leaf parsley
3 garlic cloves, finely chopped
1 pound imported penne rigate
4 artichokes, trimmed, cut into slivers, and kept in acidulated water
$1/4$ cup dry white wine
Freshly grated Parmesan cheese

BRING a large pot of salted water to a boil.

Meanwhile, in a large sauté pan, **COMBINE** the olive oil, parsley, and garlic. Sauté over medium-low heat until the parsley is bright green, 3 to 4 minutes. Add the pasta to the boiling water.

DRAIN the artichoke slivers. Add to the sauté pan along with the white wine and salt to taste. Stir to cover the artichokes with the parsley mixture. Cook over medium-low heat until the artichokes are tender, about 5 minutes.

When the pasta is cooked al dente, **DRAIN** it and toss with the sauce. Serve with Parmesan.

FETTUCCINE WITH SAUTÉED RADICCHIO, GRAPPA-SOAKED RAISINS, AND TRUFFLE OIL

Serves 4

This sophisticated pasta dish combines contrasting flavors and tony ingredients. As a bonus, there is raisin-flavored grappa to sip.

Sea salt
2 tablespoons unsalted butter
8 ounces Treviso or round red radicchio, cut into ribbons
8 ounces homemade or imported dried egg fettuccine
$^3/_4$ cup heavy cream
$^1/_4$ cup Golden Raisins Macerated in Grappa (page 127)
$^1/_4$ cup freshly grated Parmigiano-Reggiano cheese
Truffle oil

BRING a large pot of salted water to a boil.

HEAT the butter in a large sauté pan over low heat. Add the radicchio and cook gently until tender, about 8 minutes. Meanwhile, cook the fettuccine until just tender.

When the radicchio is tender, **ADD** the cream and raise the heat to medium.

DRAIN the pasta and add to the sauté pan along with the raisins. Lower the heat and toss the pasta with the radicchio. Let the flavors meld for 2 to 3 minutes.

Just before serving, **STIR** in half the Parmesan. Divide the pasta among individual plates topped with a little more grated Parmesan and a few drops of truffle oil.

RISOTTO WITH GREEN TOMATOES

Serves 4

Fall arrives when a crisp feeling creeps into the air and brown leaves start flying about in the wind. Tomato season is over, but green tomatoes that will never turn red remain on the vine. These green tomatoes—tart-sweet and absolutely wonderful to cook with—are featured in this special risotto.

3 tablespoons extra virgin olive oil

2 garlic cloves, finely chopped

3 tablespoons finely chopped fresh flat-leaf parsley

1^1/$_2$ pounds green tomatoes, thinly sliced

Sea salt

1^1/$_2$ cups Arborio rice

5 cups lightly salted water or vegetable broth, brought to a simmer

1^1/$_2$ teaspoons unsalted butter

^{1}/$_2$ cup almonds, lightly toasted (see page 29) and finely chopped

10 large, fresh basil leaves, torn into fragments

Freshly grated Parmesan cheese (optional)

In a medium, heavy-bottomed soup pot, **HEAT** the olive oil. Add the garlic and sauté over medium-low heat for 2 to 3 minutes. Add the parsley and cook another 4 minutes. Add the tomatoes and salt to taste, and stir well. Cook until the tomatoes start to break apart, about 10 minutes.

ADD the rice and stir for several minutes to coat the grains. Begin adding water or broth by the ladleful, stirring often until each ladleful has been almost fully absorbed. Add the next ladleful and continue until all the broth is used.

The risotto is done when the rice is moist but slightly al dente, about 16 minutes. **STIR** in the butter. Cover and let rest for a few minutes.

Before serving, **STIR** in the almonds and basil. Serve the risotto in shallow pasta bowls. It tastes fresher without Parmesan, but use if desired.

RISOTTO WITH PINK RADICCHIO AND GOLDEN BEETS

Serves 4

All the radicchios in the garden are a marvel to watch grow. The array of colors and shapes is startling, from creamy white variegated Chioggia blushed with pink to taut cylinders of deep burgundy Treviso. They are a stunning addition to the vegetable patch.

A scattering of sweet golden beets cut into jewel-like dice top the risotto, a palate-pleasing contrast to slightly bitter radicchio.

4 tablespoons ($\frac{1}{2}$ stick) unsalted butter
2 tablespoons extra virgin olive oil
$\frac{1}{4}$ medium onion, finely diced
2 cups Arborio rice
6 cups vegetable or meat broth, brought to a simmer
Sea salt
1 Chioggia or round red radicchio, cut into thin ribbons (about $1\frac{1}{2}$ cups)
Freshly grated Parmigiano-Reggiano cheese
$\frac{1}{4}$ cup finely diced cooked golden beets
Truffle oil

PLACE 1 tablespoon of the butter and all the olive oil in a heavy-bottomed 2-quart saucepan over low heat. Add the onion and cook slowly, about 10 minutes, until tender. Add the rice and stir to coat the grains.

ADD the hot broth to the rice one ladleful at a time, stirring frequently. When the liquid is absorbed, add another ladleful and repeat, stirring frequently, always over low heat. Toward the end of the cooking, taste for salt and add as needed.

Meanwhile, in a separate sauté pan, **HEAT** 2 tablespoons of the butter over low heat. Add the radicchio and stir to coat. Cook over low heat, stirring occasionally, until tender, about 5 minutes.

When the rice is al dente but still creamy, **STIR** in the radicchio. Let warm together over low heat for another 5 minutes to unite flavors.

Off the heat, **ADD** the remaining 1 tablespoon butter and Parmesan to taste and stir well.

LADLE the risotto into individual shallow pasta bowls. Top with a bit of the diced beets and a few drops of truffle oil. Serve immediately.

ARTICHOKE AND LEEK RISOTTO WITH CREAM

Serves 4

Artichokes, when just harvested, are incredibly tender. I cut them about four inches down the stem. The stem is strongly flavored, and after the thick peel is removed, cooks to the same tenderness as the artichoke hearts. I slice the stem into small pieces, put it in acidulated water, and then cook it with the slivered artichoke.

$\frac{1}{2}$ lemon
3 artichokes
2 tablespoons extra virgin olive oil
2 tablespoons unsalted butter
1 leek, white and light green parts thinly sliced into rings
2 cups Arborio rice
6 cups vegetable or meat broth, brought to a simmer
$\frac{1}{4}$ cup heavy cream
6 tablespoons freshly grated Parmigiano-Reggiano cheese

FILL a large bowl with water. Squeeze in the lemon juice. Set aside the squeezed lemon half.

SNAP back the tough outer leaves from the artichokes. Rub the cut portions with the squeezed lemon as you work. Trim some of the dark green portion at the base. Cut the artichokes in half and cut away any developed choke. Sliver the artichoke halves and submerge in the lemon water.

Meanwhile, in a heavy-bottomed 2-quart saucepan, **HEAT** the olive oil and 1 tablespoon of the butter. Add the leek, stir, and cook over low heat until tender, about 10 minutes. Drain the artichokes and stir into the leek. Cook until the artichokes are al dente, about 5 minutes.

ADD the rice and stir to coat the grains. Cook about 3 minutes. Add the broth, one ladleful at a time, allowing the rice to absorb the liquid before adding the next ladleful.

When the rice is al dente but still creamy (about 20 minutes), **REMOVE** from heat.

Off the heat, **STIR** in the remaining tablespoon butter, the cream, and the Parmesan. Ladle into shallow pasta bowls and serve immediately.

GRILLED WILD MUSHROOMS WITH WINTER SAVORY AND GARLIC

Serves 4

Try to find a source for wild mushrooms. I am lucky to have "Lorenzo, the Wild Mushroom Man," as my friend. Serve these succulent large mushrooms as you would steak, to be eaten with knife and fork, at the center of the meal. Porcini mushrooms would be ideal.

> 8 large wild mushrooms or portobellos
> Extra virgin olive oil
> Sea salt
> Freshly ground black pepper
> 2 tablespoons finely chopped fresh winter savory or thyme
> 2 garlic cloves, minced

HEAT an outdoor grill or a stove-top cast-iron ridged grill.

REMOVE the stems from the mushrooms. Wipe the caps with damp paper towels. Generously brush both sides of the mushrooms with olive oil. Season with salt and pepper to taste. Cut 2 or 3 shallow diagonal slits in the top, not the cavity, of each mushroom.

CHOP the winter savory, garlic, and 1 teaspoon salt together until it forms a coarse paste. Carefully insert a little of the paste into the slits of the mushrooms.

Carefully **RUB** the hot grill with a cloth lightly moistened with olive oil. Place the mushrooms on the grill, gill side up. Grill until the mushrooms begin to soften lightly. Turn once and grill on the other side until just tender and moist. This will take only a few minutes. Be careful not to overcook them.

TRANSFER the mushrooms to a platter and let them rest for a moment before serving with a basket of rustic bread.

RICE, CURLY ENDIVE, AND MOZZARELLA TORTA

Serves 6

Curly endive looks like a very frilly bouquet. It stands out among the larger leaves of escarole and lettuces growing in the section of one of my terraces devoted to greens. This torta is easily assembled and very satisfying.

Sea salt

1 head curly endive, leaves separated

1 cup Arborio rice

2 tablespoons unsalted butter, plus extra for buttering the pan

$^1/_4$ cup extra virgin olive oil

$^1/_2$ cup chopped onion

$^1/_4$ cup toasted unflavored dried bread crumbs

4 large eggs, lightly beaten with a fork

$^1/_2$ cup freshly grated pecorino Romano cheese

1 cup coarsely shredded mozzarella cheese

Freshly ground black pepper

PREHEAT the oven to 425°F.

BRING a large pot of salted water to a boil. Plunge the endive into the water and cook until the leaves are tender, about 5 minutes. Remove the leaves with a large slotted spoon. Place in a bowl to cool.

ADD the rice to the boiling endive-flavored water. Cook at a lively simmer until the rice is cooked but still a little al dente, about 16 minutes. Drain and set aside.

(continued)

Meanwhile, **PLACE** 2 tablespoons of the butter and the olive oil in a sauté pan over low heat. Add the onion and cook until tender. Chop the cooked endive and add to the sauté pan. Stir over low heat to let the flavors mingle for about 5 minutes.

BUTTER a 10-inch springform pan or a baking dish of equivalent size. Coat with bread crumbs and shake off the excess. Reserve the excess crumbs.

In a bowl, **COMBINE** the rice, endive mixture, eggs, about half the pecorino, and the mozzarella. Stir well to combine and add salt and pepper to taste.

PUT the mixture in the prepared pan, level the top, and sprinkle with the remaining pecorino and bread crumbs. Bake for about 20 minutes, or until slightly firm to the touch and golden on top.

SERVE warm or at room temperature, cut into wedges.

TORTA SALATA WITH ERBETTE

Serves 6

Erbette, also called *biete da taglio,* is a ribless cut-and-come-again form of Swiss chard. Its tenderness is similar to spinach but without the residual taste of spinach's oxalic acid content that so often spoils my enjoyment of spinach. Erbette has a pleasing sweet vegetal aftertaste on the tongue.

With many tender ribless chard leaves in the fall garden, I use them to assemble this lovely savory tart.

Marjoram is one of the sweetest of the garden herbs. Use it in moderation.

2 tablespoons extra virgin olive oil

1 teaspoon finely chopped fresh marjoram

2 tablespoons chopped fresh flat-leaf parsley

4 cups erbette leaves, blanched, drained, and chopped

Sea salt

Coarsely ground black pepper

2 large eggs, lightly beaten with a fork

1 pound whole-milk ricotta, well drained

3 tablespoons freshly grated Parmigiano-Reggiano cheese

Unsalted butter

Toasted bread crumbs

PREHEAT the oven to 375°F.

HEAT the olive oil in a medium sauté pan. Add the marjoram and parsley and sauté for 2 minutes, or until fragrant. Add the greens, season with salt and pepper, and sauté for 2 to 3 minutes. Let cool. *(continued)*

COMBINE the eggs and ricotta in a large bowl. Fold in the greens and Parmesan. Add salt and pepper to taste.

COAT a baking dish with butter and bread crumbs. Place the mixture in the pan and level the top. Bake for 45 minutes, or until firm and light golden.

LORENZO THE WILD MUSHROOM MAN'S MUSHROOM STUFATO

Serves 4

The mushrooms do not come from my garden but are a gift from a retired Italian man, Lorenzo, who supplies my local trattoria. He gathers them from the wild and knows just where to go and which ones to pick. His freshly picked wild mushrooms have a pronounced deep woodsy flavor and crisp texture. I add an assortment of the tomatoes remaining in my fall garden to the mushrooms in this stew.

> **2 pounds assorted fresh wild mushrooms, or a mix of cremini, portobello, and shiitake mushrooms**
> **¼ cup extra virgin olive oil**
> **1 small onion, finely diced**
> **2 garlic cloves, finely chopped**
> **1 teaspoon chopped fresh thyme**
> **Sea salt**
> **Freshly ground black pepper**
> **2 cups peeled, seeded, and chopped tomatoes**
> **4 slices rustic bread, toasted**

CLEAN the mushrooms with damp paper towels and remove the stems. Thickly slice the mushrooms.

COMBINE the olive oil and onion in a medium braising pan. Cook over low heat until the onion is tender, about 12 minutes. Add the garlic and thyme, and cook for 2 to 3 minutes more, but don't let the garlic brown. Add the mushrooms, raise the heat to medium, and sauté the mushrooms for a few minutes, stirring often. Season with salt and pepper to taste.

(continued)

ADD the tomatoes. Simmer, partly covered, over medium-low heat for about 15 minutes, or until the juices thicken.

To serve, **PLACE** a piece of bread on the bottom of shallow bowls and ladle the mushrooms over the top.

YOUNG FENNEL WITH BAY LEAVES AND GARLIC

Serves 4

The licorice taste and aroma of small new fennel bulbs is incredibly seductive. Infused with garlic and fresh bay leaves, this dish has an amazing depth of flavor.

8 very small fennel bulbs, feathery tops removed

2 fresh bay leaves, torn in half

4 garlic cloves, cut in half

3 tablespoons extra virgin olive oil

PREHEAT the oven to 400°F.

PLACE all the ingredients with ¼ cup water in a baking dish with a cover. Stir the ingredients to combine. Bake, covered, for 20 minutes. Uncover and bake for an additional 10 minutes, or until tender.

TURNIP TIELLA

Serves 4

The skin on young turnips is very tender and does not require the deep peeling necessary on larger turnips. This *tiella*, or gratin, is simple to assemble, but the finished dish is divinely good.

3 tablespoons extra virgin olive oil, plus extra for the baking dish
1 pound small turnips, peeled and thinly sliced
1 onion, thinly sliced
1 garlic clove, minced
Sea salt
Freshly ground black pepper
1 teaspoon chopped fresh thyme
Freshly grated Parmigiano-Reggiano cheese

PREHEAT the oven to 375°F. Oil a baking dish.

COMBINE the turnips and onion in a large bowl. Add the garlic, salt and pepper to taste, and the thyme and mix well.

SPREAD the vegetable mixture in the baking dish, drizzle with the 3 tablespoons olive oil, and pour ½ cup water over it. Bake, covered, for 20 minutes. Stir once with a spatula during the baking so that the vegetables on top are moved to the bottom of the dish. Uncover, toss, and bake uncovered for another 20 minutes. When the turnips are uniformly tender, generously sprinkle Parmesan on top and bake for another 5 minutes. Let rest for 5 minutes and serve.

WHOLE TREVISO RADICCHIO IN BROWNED BUTTER

Serves 4

Treviso radicchio is one of the best red radicchios for cooking. Its elongated, rich burgundy-colored leaves are incredibly succulent. It is often grilled, a delicious way to savor its qualities.

Here, I've slowly cooked the whole heads in water and butter until the water evaporates and the butter browns a little, adding a nutty quality. Serve alone as a first course to fully experience the extraordinary flavor and texture.

> 4 large, firm heads Treviso or round red radicchio
> 6 tablespoons unsalted butter
> Sea salt

TRIM the roots from the radicchio, leaving enough to keep the heads intact.

PLACE the butter in a sauté pan just large enough to contain the radicchio in one layer. Melt the butter over low heat. Arrange the radicchio in the pan and gently turn them in the butter to coat.

COOK over low heat for 5 minutes, turning the heads occasionally to cook on all sides. Add ½ cup water and salt to taste. Raise the heat to a simmer. Cover and cook for about 10 minutes. The radicchio should be tender but hold its shape.

UNCOVER the pan and raise the heat to medium-high. Cook until the water evaporates completely and the butter turns golden brown. Serve immediately.

SWISS CHARD AL FORNO

Serves 4

Swiss chard leaves with thick, succulent ribs are an eye-catching sight among the many greens in the garden. The plump ribs are delicious and should be savored, never discarded.

> 5 tablespoons unsalted butter, plus extra for buttering the pan
> About 2 pounds Swiss chard
> Sea salt
> 1/2 cup freshly grated Grana Padano cheese
> 1/4 cup dried bread crumbs

PREHEAT the oven to 375°F. Butter a gratin dish.

TRIM the ends of the chard. Strip the leaves from the stalks. Coarsely chop the leaves. Cut the stalks crosswise into 3 pieces.

PLACE the stalks in a large sauté pan. Add just enough water to cover the stalks; season with salt to taste. Simmer, uncovered, until just tender, about 10 minutes. Remove with a slotted spoon and place on a plate. Add the chopped leaves to the water remaining in the pan and cook until tender, about 5 minutes. Set aside.

MELT 4 tablespoons of the butter in a sauté pan. Add the stalks, leaves, and any remaining liquid and gently toss in the butter. Cook over low heat for several minutes or until the chard is glossy with butter and the water has evaporated.

ARRANGE half of the stalks and greens in the prepared dish. Scatter half of the cheese over the top. Add the remaining Swiss chard and level the top. Sprinkle with the remaining cheese and the bread crumbs. Dot with the remaining tablespoon of butter. Bake, uncovered, for 15 to 20 minutes, or until a golden crust forms over the top.

PIZZA WITH RED AND GREEN TOMATOES

Makes 4 individual pizzas

Fall is a season of change. In this pizza, the last of the ripe red tomatoes are combined with the remaining green tomatoes never to ripen. With fresh basil still fragrant, it is a tribute to summer during that glorious period called Indian summer.

To keep the tomato experience pure, there is no mozzarella in this pizza.

Pizza Dough (page 58)
Sea salt
2 large ripe tomatoes, sliced
2 large green tomatoes, sliced
Extra virgin olive oil
2 garlic cloves, thinly sliced
$^1/_2$ teaspoon dried oregano
Fresh basil leaves

When the 4 balls of dough have rested for about half an hour, **PLACE** a baking stone on the top rack of the oven and turn the heat to 500°F. Let the stone heat for at least 30 minutes. Half an hour before shaping the dough, salt the tomato slices and drain on paper towels. Wipe excess moisture from the tomatoes.

SHAPE the pizzas according to the directions on page 57. Drizzle each pizza with 1 tablespoon olive oil and spread over the surface. Layer the tomatoes, alternating red and green slices, to cover the top. Sprinkle with a quarter of the garlic and a pinch of oregano.

BAKE as directed on page 58. Remove from the oven and drizzle with olive oil. Tear fragments of basil over the top and serve.

PANINI WITH ITALIAN PEPPERS AND PROVOLONE

Serves 2

If you are unable to grow these peppers in your garden, seek them out in markets. You'll be delighted you did.

2 or 3 Italian frying peppers
3 tablespoons extra virgin olive oil
Slices of imported provolone cheese, enough to cover 2 slices of bread
4 slices rustic bread

SPLIT the peppers in half lengthwise and remove the seeds. Cut into thick strips. Warm the olive oil in a medium sauté pan. Add the peppers and sauté over medium-high heat until tender and the skin is slightly blistered. Set aside.

ARRANGE the provolone on two slices of bread. Distribute the peppers along with the oil and juices over the cheese.

COVER with the other bread slices. Gently press down with the palm of your hand to bind the ingredients. No salt is necessary since the cheese is salty and strongly flavored.

DRIED FIG AND TOASTED ALMOND "PESTO"

Makes approximately 1 cup

When I have an overabundance of figs, I dry some to prepare this pesto. This is wonderful served with cheese at the end of a meal in late fall.

1/2 pound fresh figs
1/2 cup almonds, toasted (see page 29) and coarsely chopped
1 teaspoon anise seed

ARRANGE the figs on a baking sheet lined with parchment paper. Place in a 200°F oven until the figs lose moisture but are still a little plump, about 2 hours. Cut away the stems and finely chop the figs.

ADD the almonds and anise seed and continue to chop until the mixture turns into a coarse paste. Store in the refrigerator in a jar with a tight-fitting lid.

SERVE as an accompaniment to cheeses at the end of a meal. Or enjoy the pesto on its own, spread on crostini.

CANDIED WHOLE KUMQUATS

Makes 1 pint

I don't have the intense heat of the Mediterranean, so only certain citrus fruits will grow in my garden. Kumquats, because they are small and contain just a very few drops of tart juice, do well in my climate. This small oval fruit has brilliant orange skin that surprisingly, in spite of the tart juice, is quite sweet. When candied whole, they turn into translucent orange jewels. Use the candied kumquats in my recipe for panna cotta on page 130.

1 pound firm but deeply colored ripe kumquats
3¹/₂ cups sugar, plus ¹/₂ cup extra for coating the fruit

PLACE the kumquats in a saucepan. Cover with cold water and bring to a boil. Gently simmer the kumquats for approximately 10 minutes. Drain well on paper towels.

COMBINE the 3½ cups sugar and 2 cups water in a heavy-bottomed saucepan and bring to a boil; simmer until the sugar is dissolved. Add the kumquats to the sugar syrup, lower the heat, and simmer until the fruits look almost transparent, 15 to 20 minutes depending on the size of the fruit. Let the kumquats cool in the syrup.

PLACE a wire rack over a baking sheet. Remove the cooled fruits from the syrup using a slotted spoon and arrange on the rack. Reserve the syrup. As the syrup drains off, the fruits will dry, a process that can take several hours or as long as 24 hours.

SPREAD the ½ cup sugar on a plate. Roll the kumquats in sugar to coat them. Pack the candied kumquats in a jar with a screwtop lid and store in the pantry. Keep the reserved syrup in a jar with a tight-fitting lid in the refrigerator.

USE the fruits as a topping for panna cotta, ice cream, or other desserts. The syrup tastes sweet and kumquat-y and can be used either alone or with the fruit as a topping for desserts.

GOLDEN RAISINS MACERATED IN GRAPPA

Living so close to the wine country, I've been able to gather grapes dried on the vine. The grappa-infused raisins are plump and ready to use in about an hour. But when left in the pantry for up to a month, the grappa becomes a flavorful drink, mellowed by the sweet taste of raisins.

The raisins can be spooned over ice cream or even used in savory dishes; see page 105 for a pasta recipe using grappa-soaked raisins.

$1/2$ cup golden raisins
Grappa

PLACE the raisins in a small glass jar with a tight-fitting lid. Cover the raisins generously with grappa. Let macerate for at least 1 hour. Store in the pantry for up to a month.

SAFFRON PEARS POACHED IN WINE

Serves 4

Giovanni and Ginetta have a pear tree in their Italian garden. I have watched it grow ever since they planted it after I moved into my home. It produces the nicest little pears, which they kindly share with me.

Poached in saffron-tinted wine, the whole pears look almost unreal—so golden! Make sure to cook the pears until just al dente to retain their texture.

    1/2 lemon
    4 small pears
    1 bottle white wine, such as Pinot Grigio
    1 cup sugar
    Pinch of saffron threads

SQUEEZE the lemon half into a bowl of water. Use a vegetable peeler to peel the pears, leaving the fruit whole and stems intact. Cut a small slice off the bottom of each pear so it will stay upright. Plunge each peeled pear into the lemon water to prevent discoloration.

POUR enough of the wine to cover the pears in a saucepan large enough to contain the pears snugly in an upright position. Add the sugar. Crumble the saffron threads into the liquid. Bring to a boil, then reduce the heat to a simmer.

COOK the pears in the wine until al dente, about 10 minutes. Check one pear with a thin wooden skewer at regular intervals to prevent overcooking.

REMOVE pears from the liquid. Boil the remaining liquid until syrupy. Let cool. Gently roll each pear in the syrup until golden. Serve whole pears at room temperature.

PANNA COTTA WITH CANDIED KUMQUATS

Serves 6

Panna cotta is the essence of fresh cream. I've added only a touch of vanilla flavoring to bring out its natural sweet flavor without intruding on the freshness.

With candied kumquats in my pantry, I find that a garnish of these sparkling gems along with a drizzle of the kumquat syrup serves to keep the palate fresh and lively while savoring the richness of the cream. You can also serve panna cotta with a topping of finely diced fresh fruit or a drizzle of best-quality balsamic vinegar.

> 2 cups whole milk
> 1 envelope unflavored gelatin
> 1 cup heavy cream
> $\frac{1}{4}$ cup sugar
> 1 teaspoon vanilla extract
> Almond oil
> Candied Whole Kumquats with syrup (page 126)

POUR ½ cup of the milk into a saucepan. Sprinkle the gelatin evenly over the milk and let stand 5 minutes to soften. Over low heat, stir well until the gelatin dissolves completely, about 5 minutes. Stir in the remaining milk, the cream, and sugar, and cook until small bubbles form around the edges of the pan.

REMOVE from the heat. Stir in the vanilla and let cool a little. Use almond oil to coat six ½-cup ramekins. Pour the mixture into the prepared molds. Refrigerate, covered with a sheet of parchment paper, until firm.

UNMOLD onto individual serving dishes. Serve cold or cool accompanied by a garnish of candied kumquats and a drizzle of kumquat syrup.

WINTER

IT IS NIGHTTIME NOW and outside my bedroom window, warm in my bed, I can see the outline of the bay tree I carefully coaxed into its current plump columnar shape. Before, it was an ungainly half-bush/half-tree. Now it is a contoured architectural component of the garden. When the bay leaves are torn in half, they release their essential oil, which smells of lemon and vanilla, with a warm herbal undertone. They go into many of my dishes. I notice that the tall cypress trees are swaying in the wind. The rest of the garden is bathed in darkness.

When I wake up, it is early morning and the light is at that in-between point where night turns to day. My eyes naturally turn toward the garden. It has rained hard during the night, our first storm of the cold season. The dark green leaves shimmer and shine; the cypresses sparkle with glassy beads of water that refract the pale winter sun.

A potted papyrus plant is on the balcony outside the kitchen. Each long stem is topped with sparkler-like bursts of thin filaments. When I peek outside, its leaves now hang limp like wet hair on those five- and six-foot stems swaying precariously in the wind.

I bundle up and go into the garden. The light is brightening, but only winter bright. I take stock of how the garden has reacted to this rainy assault. I'm especially concerned about standing water. Mediterranean plants do not like their roots to sit in water. I check to make sure there are no pools of standing water on any of the seven elevations of terraced land. Since it is only the first substantial rain, mercifully all the water has been absorbed by my thirsty plants. My effort to create soil with good drainage has worked, at least so far.

The euphorbia, with bluish-green pointed leaves on long stems, is growing at a fast pace. In fact, it has been in constant need of pruning. I'm filled with anticipation. In late spring and summer, huge clusters of frothy lime green blossoms will top each woody stem. The euphorbia is set between two cypress trees on the left side of the long back terrace of land. I can imagine a time when the sun will backlight the color and turn the very air surrounding the plant a glowing lime green, a stark contrast to the deep, dark green of cypresses. These euphorbia blossoms will be so splendid they will rival the mophead hydrangeas in the garden.

My striped agave would prefer no water at all. A small reservoir of rain sits in the heart of its snakelike leaves. The water creates a reflecting pool with light playing on its surface. The succulent, leathery leaves are shiny and wet, but the thick-satin texture allows water to slide right off, preventing rot. I planted the agave in one of the rockiest, meanest parts of the garden, knowing this plant prefers to struggle to survive. Natural rainfall and underground springs that run deep under our neighborhood hillside provide more than enough water for most of my sturdiest plants.

The winter garden is radiant, cool, and fragrant with the scent of rain. Each plant, small or large, has taken on a different but equally enthralling winter personality. My skin feels soft and moist in the cool mist. I bend to smell and touch the artemisia's fine tracery of leaves, its sweet sea-salt scent. It is a bouquet of ice-colored lace.

The parthenocissus, a creeping vine, looks like grape leaves. It was supposed to be semideciduous. It has dropped all its autumn-colored leaves of flame, rust, magenta, amber, fuchsia, and pomegranate and they lie in small pathetic piles at the base of each plant. What remains is a trail of stems up the garden walls. I'll have to wait until early spring for it to put out tiny new green leaflets. Leaf mulch is good for the soil. As it decomposes, it puts nutrients back into the earth. But to protect the plant from disease, I rake the leaves away about six inches or so from the base, depending on the size of the plant.

The fig tree was still in leafy splendor until early December. It is now completely devoid of leaves. Twisted and crinkly brown ones have fallen to the ground. Green figs that will never ripen are starting to rot on the branches. I need to remove these to discourage pests from invading the tree. The tree's growth has been fast. It leans precariously, staked loosely to encourage the roots to cling deep into the earth. Staking too rigidly keeps the tree dependent on the stake instead of its own root system for stability and strength.

Winter savory and oregano are still vigorous, unfazed by California's winter assault. Less pungent and aromatic, the herbs still have an aura of sultry summer, even in the cold air.

The lemon tree's normally shiny leaves are even shinier, the golden fruits speckled with droplets of water. My first and most precious Meyer lemon tree started out in a cramped pot on the upstairs balcony, the hottest spot when the garden was still the forest primeval. It was welcomed into the earth when the blazing sun emerged after the giant Christmas trees were cut down. It is laden with glossy, green to yellow fruit, fifty, perhaps, sixty, in all. A scattering of sweet-smelling, starry-shaped blossoms will later transform themselves into more fruit. Without heat, the green fruits ripen slowly but steadily. The lemon tree was the first plant to make

its way down from the sunny balcony into my Italian garden, so it holds a special place in my heart.

The recent rain and "gale force" winds, as we half-jokingly refer to them, knocked over my tightly furled big red umbrella, heavy pedestal and all. I should have brought it in last month, so I'll blame myself, not the wind, for that. The umbrella remained intact but broke off a large branch of one of the mature rosemary plants. I was just about to trim it into a conical shape to match its twin neighbor on the other side of the path in the herb and fragrance terrace. I will attempt to give it some semblance of shape when I return to the garden to work. But first the mud needs to dry.

In deepest winter, the jasmine is in full bloom, garlands draped high across the terrace walls. Those indomitable hollyhocks are still budding and blossoming on stilt-like, sturdy stalks. They swayed and bent in the wind, but did not snap or splinter—amazingly resilient for such an exquisite blossoming plant.

Weeding continues to be a theme. Why weed with rain, and more rain predicted on the way? When the soil is moist, it is easier to weed. Every oxalis removed right down to its little ball of stored energy at the base of the taproot stops a network of roots that will turn into other weeds—hundreds, maybe thousands. I use a screwdriver or a special long, narrow weeding tool for this job. I am particularly careful near the base of trees and plants. A few weeds do less harm than damaging the roots of a tree.

When the soil is no longer pure mud and dries up enough, I'll heavily scatter wild arugula seeds and Italian parsley in the terrace with the fig tree, the section of garden that gets the most sustained heat for the greatest part of the year. The sun and reflected heat off the "Roman" walls raise the temperature in the terrace.

I run my hand against this wall and once again feel the soft, velvety bands of green moss among the ripples of stone. The last of the intensely magenta bracts of the colored leaves of bougainvillea are drying to ethereal shades of paler and paler magenta until they turn to parchment and flutter to the ground. My "problem child" bougainvillea did produce some Mediterranean color, and I hope for better days ahead for my plant.

I arrange the citron fruits from my neighbor across the street in a big straw basket. I stand back to admire them. Large, bumpy, pocked, yellow, and sweet smelling, I enjoy the arrangement for a long time. But when my desire to taste them overcomes my visual pleasure, I begin to use them in every way I can imagine. An Italian neighbor around the corner does not let me pass by the house without offering bitter greens or tart little apples he's gathered from his brother's land in Sonoma. Ginetta tosses over the fence a tightly furled head of Treviso radicchio she pulled out of the ground, thick central root and all. So beautiful, I put it in a vase. But as with the citrons, I can't resist cooking the succulent burgundy chicory.

Our winter can become ferocious on occasion. No snow or sleet, no ice storms. But we are soft people. When it rains hard, it does just that. Today, the rain seems torrential to me, and the wind, wild. It is a *temporale*, a bad storm, at least by San Francisco standards.

Looking out the kitchen window from my watch-guard position, I'm truly horrified by what I see. Could it be that the winds are so strong they have toppled over my huge pot of trailing hot pink geraniums? I thought it was securely settled on a strong pedestal—my prize geraniums, admired by all, especially myself. I've been tending the plant so carefully. But I've learned, all right. Geraniums are hardy. I will wait until the storm is over and ask someone to help me lift up the heavy pot. I have faith it will continue to blossom.

In this Italian garden of mine, I use time-honored methods developed over centuries. I've listened keenly to advice from my friend in Italy, Pino, and my dear neighbors Ginetta and Giovanni. My own research has taught me to respect the cycle of seasons. I've learned to accept lessons of what will or won't grow and use everything in the garden—parsley stems to add to broths, arugula blossoms in salads and frittatas—augmented by generous offerings from neighbors. I reciprocate with a full heart with whatever I have to offer.

ANTIPASTI · *Starters*

Ceci Crisped in Hot Herbed Extra Virgin Olive Oil   139
Sun-dried Principe Borghese Tomatoes Wrapped in Capocollo Salame   140
Warm Crostini Topped with Truffled Anchovy Butter and Crispy Sage Leaves   141

INSALATE · *Salads*

Winter Caprese   143
Pan di Zucchero Salad with Mint, Orange Zest, and Hard-cooked Egg   144
Lamon Bean Salad   146
Potato and Escarole Salad   147

MINESTRE · *Soups*

Farro Soup with Ricotta Salata   148
Zuppa della Salute   149
Tubetti and Umbrian Lentil Soup   150
Passato of Cannellini Beans and Cima di Rapa   151

PASTA

Fettuccine with Wild Mushrooms and Winter Herbs   152
Fettuccine with Tomato and Truffled Anchovy Butter   154
Ditalini with Chickpeas and Tomatoes al Forno   156

RISOTTO

Risotto with Orange and Lemon   157

PIATTI FORTI · *Main Dishes*

Vegetable Crespelle Topped with Herb Besciamella, al Forno   159
Herb and Parmesan Custards with Truffle Oil   163
Sformato of Young Cauliflower and Herb-infused Besciamella   165
Sformato of Green Cauliflower and Goat Cheese   167

VERDURE · *Vegetables*

Warm Lamon Beans with Grilled Radicchio   169

Cima di Rapa with Black Olives and Fresh Bay Leaves   171

Baked Chickpeas in Butter with Rosemary Sprigs   172

Broccoli Rabe in Lemon Cream   174

Whole Escarole Stuffed with Currants, Sun-dried Tomatoes, and Toasted Pine Nuts   175

Pugliese Catalogna Chicory with Red Onion and Salame   177

PIZZA AND PANINI

Pizza with Potato and Arugula   178

Panini with Greens, Black Olives, and Ricotta   180

CONDIMENTI · *Condiments*

Green Olive and Meyer Lemon Relish   182

Red Carrots sott'Aceto with Hot Red Peppers   183

Red Wine Sciroppo   184

DESSERTS AND GELATO

Vanilla Custard with Red Wine Sciroppo   185

Bitter Orange Gelato with Mint Leaves   186

· Winter Garden ·

Alloro · European bay

Carota rossa · red carrots

Cavolfiore · cauliflower

Cicoria Catalogna Pugliese · long-leafed chicory

Cicoria Pan di Zucchero · pale green chicory

Cicoria rossa di Treviso · Treviso radicchio

Cicoria variegato di Castelfranco · variegated cream and pink Castelfranco radicchio

Cima di rapa · broccoli rabe

Fagioli rampicante Lamon · climbing Lamon (borlotti) beans

Indivia scarola · escarole

Kumquats

Limone · Meyer lemon

Menta · mint

Origano · Italian oregano

Prezzemolo comune · small flat-leaf Italian parsley

Prezzemolo gigante di Napoli · large flat-leaf Neapolitan parsley

Ravanelli · radishes

Romanesco broccoli · green cauliflower

Rucola selvatica · wild arugula

Salvia officinale · sage

Spinaci · spinach

Timo · thyme

CECI CRISPED IN HOT HERBED EXTRA VIRGIN OLIVE OIL

Serves 4 to 6

Impossible to stop eating, this super high-protein chickpea antipasto is also a natural served at a party. Either place in a large basket lined with parchment paper and garnished with herb sprigs, or spoon the warm chickpeas into small serving bowls and set out for guests to nibble.

1 cup cooked chickpeas (see page 172)
$^1/_4$ cup extra virgin olive oil
2 sprigs fresh rosemary
2 sprigs fresh sage
2 sprigs fresh thyme
1 garlic clove, cut in half
$^1/_4$ cup unbleached all-purpose flour
Sea salt

SPREAD the chickpeas on a clean kitchen towel to remove surface moisture. In a large sauté pan, combine the olive oil, rosemary, sage, thyme, and garlic. Warm over low heat, stirring gently until fragrant. Remove the garlic so it does not get bitter.

DREDGE the chickpeas in flour. Shake off the excess. Raise the heat to medium. With a slotted spoon, carefully transfer the chickpeas to the hot oil and fry until light golden, about 4 minutes, shaking the pan to distribute the heat on all sides of the chickpeas. Drain well on paper towels and sprinkle with salt. Serve warm in a basket lined with parchment paper.

SUN-DRIED PRINCIPE BORGHESE TOMATOES WRAPPED IN CAPOCOLLO SALAME

This earthy recipe speaks of southern Italy. With sun-dried tomatoes in the pantry, all you have to do is assemble the ingredients. Make as many as you want, or just one, for a quick snack.

Italians use sun-dried tomatoes primarily as an antipasto and rarely toss them into pasta sauces or salads.

Sun-dried Principe Borghese tomatoes (page 63) or sun-dried Sungold tomatoes
Slices of capocollo
Home-dried Italian oregano (page 64)
Salt-Cured Nasturtium Buds (page 66) or salt-cured capers
Red wine, if needed

LIFT the tomatoes from the oil and drain on paper towels.

ARRANGE the slices of capocollo on a cutting board. Place a sun-dried tomato in the center of each slice along with a sprinkle of oregano and nasturtium buds. Wrap the capocollo around the tomato and secure with a toothpick. Place on a serving platter.

If preparing in advance, **WRAP** the rolls tightly in several layers of cheesecloth soaked in red wine to prevent the capocollo from drying out.

WARM CROSTINI TOPPED WITH TRUFFLED ANCHOVY BUTTER AND CRISPY SAGE LEAVES

Serves 4

Crostini are a classic Italian beginning to a meal as well as a staple at parties. In a country where bread is always in the pantry and is used in myriad ways, it is only natural that thin rounds of bread would be used as a base for various toppings.

I always have a jar of truffled anchovies in the pantry so I can prepare these tasty bites on the spur of the moment. And with sage growing in a pot just outside the kitchen door, I can gather the leaves right before using to release the maximum aroma and flavor when they hit the hot oil.

Truffled anchovies are available at specialty markets.

1 small baguette, cut into 12 thin rounds
4 tablespoons ($^1/_2$ stick) unsalted butter, at room temperature
4 meaty truffled anchovy fillets, drained on paper towels
Extra virgin olive oil
12 medium sage leaves

PREHEAT the oven to 350°F.

ARRANGE the bread rounds on a baking sheet without overlapping the bread. Place in the oven. When the tops are golden brown, turn them over to lightly brown the other side. The crostini should be just crisp, but not dried out. Total time will be about 6 minutes. Remove the crostini from the oven and place on a serving plate.

Meanwhile, **PLACE** the butter in a small bowl. Chop the anchovies finely, then mash them into a paste, using a fork to make a uniformly smooth texture. Mix the anchovies into the butter until well combined. Set aside.

(continued)

In a medium sauté pan, **HEAT** enough olive oil to cover the bottom of the pan by about ¼ inch. Toss several sage leaves at a time into the hot oil and fry until crisp, just 1 or 2 minutes. Drain on paper towels. Continue until all the sage leaves are cooked.

SPREAD a little of the truffled anchovy butter on each crostini. Top with a crisp sage leaf and serve immediately.

WINTER CAPRESE

Serves 4

Even winter can't escape a playful take on this summer staple. The combination of toasted hazelnuts, slivered radicchio, and the zest of brilliant oranges has a warming feel and is true to the season. The final *tocco*, the touch, of truffle oil makes the wintry picture complete.

Four 4-ounce fresh mozzarella balls, brought to room temperature
1 small head Treviso or round red radicchio
Sea salt
6 to 8 tablespoons extra virgin olive oil
$^{1}/_{2}$ cup hazelnuts, lightly toasted, loose skins rubbed off, and
    coarsely chopped (see page 29)
Zest of 1 small orange
Truffle oil

SLICE the mozzarella into rounds. If very moist, drain on a kitchen towel.

CORE the radicchio and separate the leaves. Arrange the leaves on a large serving plate, reserving a few for garnish. Cover the leaves with slightly overlapping slices of mozzarella. Season with salt.

DRIZZLE olive oil evenly over the mozzarella. Sprinkle the hazelnuts and orange zest over the cheese. Sliver the remaining radicchio leaves and sprinkle over the top. Just before serving, add a very light drizzle of truffle oil.

PAN DI ZUCCHERO SALAD WITH MINT, ORANGE ZEST, AND HARD-COOKED EGG

Serves 4

The exquisite pale green chicory called Pan di Zucchero, so silky and delicate, is unusually formed with leaves that wrap tightly around each other. It has just the right touch of pleasing tonic pungence. In this must-try salad, the perfume of just-picked mint and a touch of bitter orange juice accent the Pan di Zucchero magnificently.

The oranges come from my next-door neighbors. They are a bit sour since we lack the intense heat for the fruit sugars to develop. I love them, though, so my neighbors give me buckets of fruit that would otherwise be discarded.

The egg adds beauty and substance, transforming the salad into a light and nourishing main dish lunch offering.

1 large Pan di Zucchero chicory or tender inner leaves of escarole

$1/4$ cup extra virgin olive oil

$1/4$ cup fresh-squeezed bitter orange juice (or add a few drops of lemon juice to sweet orange juice to create a tart flavor)

Sea salt

Zest of $1/4$ large orange, in fine strips

Large handful (about 20) small mint leaves, slivered, with a few whole leaves set aside for garnish

Coarsely ground black pepper

2 hard-cooked large eggs, quartered

SEPARATE the chicory leaves and tear them into bite-size pieces directly into a large, shallow serving bowl.

In a small bowl, COMBINE the olive oil, orange juice, and salt. Lightly beat with a fork for a minute or so to blend ingredients.

DRIZZLE the dressing over the greens and gently toss to coat. Scatter the orange zest and mint over the top and toss very briefly. Grind pepper over the top and toss again. Garnish with the remaining whole mint leaves. Arrange the egg quarters around the edge of the serving dish and season them with a touch of salt and pepper.

LAMON BEAN SALAD

Serves 6

A variety of borlotti bean comes from the town of Lamon in northern Italy. This nutty-tasting bean can be cooked fresh from the pod or dried and cooked. Naturally, the fresh beans take much less time to cook, are incredibly creamy, and have meltingly tender skins. The characteristic almost chestnutlike flavor and texture make Lamon beans irresistible.

Vinegar or lemon would intrude on the flavor of the bean. Use only olive oil as the dressing.

Radishes grow all year round in the garden in mild climates.

3 cups cooked Lamon (borlotti) or pinto beans (see page 169)
6 tablespoons extra virgin olive oil
Sea salt
16 young radishes, thinly sliced
$\frac{1}{4}$ cup pitted oil-cured black olives, coarsely chopped
$\frac{1}{4}$ cup coarsely chopped fresh flat-leaf parsley

PLACE the beans in a shallow serving bowl. Add olive oil and salt to taste and toss gently so as not to crush the beans. Let rest at room temperature for 30 minutes or longer to allow flavors to mellow.

Just before serving, ADD the radishes, olives, and parsley, gently tossing the ingredients two or three times only. Taste for salt and add more if needed.

POTATO AND ESCAROLE SALAD

Serves 4

Escarole is at its peak during the cold months. Although it is often cooked, the pale leaves of young escarole are tender and crisp, excellent for salads.

The salad can be served right away, but it can also rest for a while. The escarole wilts a bit and will lose its crunch, but the salad will taste just as good and acquire a slightly different character.

3 medium yellow-fleshed potatoes, boiled until just tender
Sea salt
1 teaspoon home-dried Italian oregano (page 64)
1 heaping tablespoon Salt-cured Nasturtium Buds (page 66) or salt-cured capers
3 meaty salt-cured anchovy fillets, salt scraped off, coarsely chopped
¼ cup extra virgin olive oil
2 tablespoons red wine vinegar
1 small head tender escarole

PEEL the potatoes as soon as they are cool enough to handle. Cut into medium dice. Place on a serving platter and sprinkle with salt. Add the oregano, nasturtium buds, and anchovies. Drizzle with olive oil and toss gently. Sprinkle with the vinegar and toss again. Set aside and let rest for at least 30 minutes for flavors to mellow.

Meanwhile, SEPARATE the leaves of the escarole. Just before serving, tear the leaves into bite-size pieces and toss with the seasoned potatoes. Taste for salt and serve.

FARRO SOUP WITH RICOTTA SALATA

Serves 4

Farro is an ancient grain that has been spared from the meddling hands of modern agriculture. It is basically the same grain that the Romans grew as one of their staple foods. Recently, it has resurfaced.

In now prosperous Italy, humble farro has become extremely *di moda*—fashionably chic.

  2 cups farro
  3 tablespoons extra virgin olive oil, plus extra for drizzling
  ½ cup finely diced onion
  1 cup finely diced carrots
  1 cup finely diced celery
  Sea salt
  ¾ cup coarsely chopped fresh flat-leaf parsley
  Ricotta salata

PLACE the farro in a soup pot with water to cover by 3 to 4 inches. Bring to a boil. Cook at a gentle simmer for 30 to 45 minutes, or until the farro is tender but holds its shape well.

Meanwhile, **PLACE** the olive oil, onion, carrots, and celery in a sauté pan. Cook over low heat until the vegetables are tender.

ADD the vegetables and juices to the soup pot and stir to combine, adding salt to taste. Cook an additional 5 to 10 minutes. Stir the parsley into the soup at the last minute.

LADLE soup into shallow soup bowls and shred long strands of ricotta salata over the top.

ZUPPA DELLA SALUTE

Serves 4

This nourishing soup practically makes itself. It is perfect for those times when one feels slightly under the weather and hasn't the energy to spend on cooking.

Little green spinach leaves picked in the garden, sweet and tender, a few eggs, and slices of dried bread combine to make a tonic for the body. *Salute* means health, and this soup promotes health.

> **Sea salt**
> **About 1 pound very small spinach leaves, well washed**
> **2 to 3 large eggs, lightly beaten with a fork**
> **4 thick slices day-old bread, drizzled with extra virgin olive oil**
> **Freshly grated pecorino Romano cheese**

BRING 3 cups water to a boil. Add a pinch of salt and the spinach.

LOWER the heat and simmer, uncovered, until the spinach is bright green and tender, 3 to 4 minutes. Taste for salt and add more as needed. Remember that the pecorino is salty.

REMOVE from heat and pour the beaten eggs into the soup in a thin stream, whisking constantly. The eggs will form strands.

PLACE the bread slices in shallow soup bowls. Ladle the soup over the top and sprinkle with pecorino. Let rest a moment before serving so the bread can absorb some broth.

TUBETTI AND UMBRIAN LENTIL SOUP

Serves 4

Umbrian lentils are very small and flavorful. If unavailable, use market lentils. This satisfying winter soup turns bright green thanks to its generous helping of chopped parsley.

1/4 cup extra virgin olive oil
1 onion, coarsely chopped
2 celery stalks, thinly sliced
3 canned San Marzano or other plum tomatoes (homemade or purchased), seeded and chopped
3/4 cup Umbrian lentils
Freshly ground black pepper
2 large handfuls of chopped fresh flat-leaf parsley
1/2 cup imported tubetti
Sea salt

HEAT the olive oil in a heavy-bottomed soup pot. Add the onion and cook over medium heat until the onion begins to soften. Add the celery and tomatoes. Stir well and continue to cook for approximately 5 minutes. Add 4 cups water, the lentils, pepper to taste, and half the parsley.

BRING to a boil, reduce heat to a gentle simmer, and cook until the lentils are tender, about 20 minutes. Add water if necessary. Approximately 5 minutes before serving, add the pasta and remaining parsley and salt to taste. Cook at a low simmer, stirring frequently, until the pasta is al dente. Ladle into shallow soup bowls and serve.

PASSATO OF CANNELLINI BEANS AND CIMA DI RAPA

Serves 4

This *passato* is a coarse puree of white beans accented with the great flavor of chopped broccoli rabe (*cima di rapa*). I was a fanatic fan of this vegetable long before I began growing it. I watch its progress as it emerges from the earth, waiting impatiently to cook it in all sorts of ways.

> ¼ cup extra virgin olive oil, plus extra for drizzling
> 4 garlic cloves, finely chopped
> ¼ cup chopped fresh flat-leaf parsley
> 3 cups cooked cannellini beans (page 169)
> 1 pound broccoli rabe, coarsely chopped
> Sea salt

COMBINE 2 tablespoons of the olive oil, half the garlic, and all the parsley in a medium saucepan. Cook over medium-low heat for about 3 minutes, or until the garlic just begins to color. Add the beans and 2 cups of water. Bring to a boil and simmer for 10 minutes. Use a potato masher to create a coarse puree.

While the beans are cooking, **PLACE** the remaining 2 tablespoons olive oil and remaining garlic in a saucepan over low heat and cook until the garlic begins to color, about 2 minutes. Add the broccoli rabe and stir well. Add 3 cups water and salt to taste, and simmer for 15 minutes, or until the greens are tender and the broth is flavorful.

ADD the broccoli rabe and broth to the beans and stir to combine. Taste for salt and adjust the seasoning if necessary.

To serve, **LADLE** the soup into individual bowls and finish with a drizzle of extra virgin olive oil.

FETTUCCINE WITH WILD MUSHROOMS AND WINTER HERBS

Serves 2 to 4

Winter-hardy herbs such as rosemary, sage, and winter savory bring out the woodsy flavor of mushrooms. A touch of cream adds the richness we crave during the cold months. Coffee adds additional depth of flavor, and a hint of mystery.

    2 tablespoons unsalted butter
    2 tablespoons extra virgin olive oil
    $1/2$ onion, finely chopped
    2 teaspoons finely chopped fresh rosemary
    1 teaspoon finely chopped fresh sage
    1 teaspoon chopped fresh winter savory
    Pinch of espresso beans ground to a fine powder
    1 pound assorted wild mushrooms, tough stems removed, wiped clean,
        and thickly sliced
    Sea salt
    Freshly ground black pepper
    $1/4$ cup heavy cream
    $1/2$ pound fresh or imported dried egg fettuccine
    Freshly grated Parmigiano-Reggiano cheese

COMBINE the butter and olive oil in a large sauté pan over low heat. When the butter melts, add the onion and sauté until tender. Do not let the onion color. Stir in the rosemary, sage, winter savory, and espresso and let the flavors merge for several minutes.

ADD the mushrooms. Raise the heat to medium and sauté until the mushrooms are tender but still a bit firm. Season with salt and pepper to taste. Stir in the cream.

Meanwhile, **BRING** a large pot of salted water to a boil. Cook the fettuccine until just tender but not soft. Drain the fettuccine and quickly toss with the mushroom sauce. Serve topped with grated Parmesan.

FETTUCCINE WITH TOMATO AND TRUFFLED ANCHOVY BUTTER

Serves 4

This elegant wintry dish of golden fettuccine is scented with truffled anchovies. It is simple to make using pantry ingredients: truffled anchovies, canned San Marzano tomatoes, and high-quality imported egg fettuccine.

Use just the tomatoes, not the juice, so the sauce cooks down to a chunky jamlike consistency. The butter makes for a suave consistency and truffles always create a special-occasion feeling.

Truffled anchovies are available in small glass jars in many markets specializing in Italian products.

5 tablespoons unsalted butter, at room temperature
1 garlic clove, thinly sliced
One 28-ounce can San Marzano tomatoes, or about 10 home-canned
    sauce tomatoes, drained and seeded
Sea salt
4 truffled anchovy fillets, drained and finely chopped to a paste
½ pound imported egg fettuccine

WARM 3 tablespoons of the butter and the garlic in a large sauté pan. Cook until the garlic is soft and translucent, 3 to 4 minutes.

ADD the tomatoes by crushing them with your hands over the sauté pan to create a very coarse puree. Add just a bit of salt. Raise the heat to medium-low. Simmer the sauce, uncovered, for 10 to 12 minutes, stirring occasionally with a wooden spoon.

Meanwhile, **MASH** the remaining 2 tablespoons butter with the anchovies. Set aside.

While the sauce is simmering, **BRING** a large pot of salted water to a boil. Cook the fettuccine, stirring the pasta "nests" to separate the pasta ribbons so they cook evenly. Drain when tender but still a little al dente, and leaving some water clinging to the pasta.

TOSS the fettuccine with the tomato sauce, then stir in the truffled anchovy butter. Taste for salt. Serve immediately.

DITALINI WITH CHICKPEAS AND TOMATOES AL FORNO

Serves 4

My father loved ceci, or chickpeas, and often would eat a bowl of warmed chickpeas for lunch. It must be genetic, since I feel the same way.

With cooked chickpeas in the refrigerator, it is simple to prepare this baked offering. The chickpeas and pasta turn a little crisp and toasty on the surface, giving an extra depth of flavor and crunch to the finished dish.

3 tablespoons extra virgin olive oil, plus extra for drizzling
3 garlic cloves, finely diced
1/2 pound imported ditalini, cooked very al dente
2 cups cooked chickpeas (see page 172)
Sea salt
3 medium canned San Marzano tomatoes, diced
2 teaspoons dried oregano

PREHEAT the oven to 375°F.

In a large sauté pan, **COMBINE** the olive oil and garlic. Sauté over low heat until the garlic is translucent. Stir in the ditalini and chickpeas and season with salt to taste. Toss briefly to combine flavors.

TRANSFER the mixture to a large terra-cotta gratin dish about 3 inches deep. Top with the tomatoes, season with salt to taste, and sprinkle with oregano. Drizzle with olive oil to moisten the top.

BAKE for 10 to 15 minutes, or until the tomatoes have melted and the chickpeas and pasta are slightly crisp on top. Serve hot.

RISOTTO WITH ORANGE AND LEMON

Serves 4

In keeping with my resolve to base all my recipes on what grows in my garden, I have tried some unusual combinations. Usually, the results are surprisingly good.

Winter is citrus season. I've devised a risotto that relies completely on my Meyer lemons and my neighbor's not-so-sweet oranges. But it is equally delicious with common varieties of organic citrus. It tastes summery and fresh, a change of pace from deep winter flavors.

1 lemon, Meyer, if possible

1 orange

3 tablespoons unsalted butter

1 tablespoon extra virgin olive oil

$^1/_2$ onion, finely chopped

2 cups Arborio rice

$^1/_2$ cup dry white wine

6 cups mild-tasting beef broth, brought to a simmer

Sea salt

$^1/_2$ cup freshly grated Parmigiano-Reggiano cheese

Toasted almonds (see page 29), finely chopped

Mint leaves

USE a vegetable peeler to remove just the zest of the lemon and half of the orange in ribbonlike strands. Set aside. Use a zester to make fine strips of zest from the remaining orange half. Place the finer strips of orange zest in about 1 cup of boiling water for 2 to 3 minutes to remove some of the bitterness. Drain well. Dry on paper towels.

(continued)

CUT away most of the white pith from the lemon and orange, leaving a thin layer around the fruit. Very finely chop the fruit, including the attached pith and membrane. Set aside.

In a 2-quart heavy-bottomed saucepan, **PLACE** 2 tablespoons of the butter and the olive oil. Warm over low heat. Add the onion and cook gently for 8 to 10 minutes, or until meltingly tender.

ADD the rice and stir well until all the grains are glossy. Add the wine, raise the heat a little, and let the wine evaporate. Add the ribbonlike strands of citrus zest and stir.

ADD a ladleful of broth and stir until it is absorbed by the rice. Continue in this way, adding one ladleful at a time, until the rice is al dente but the risotto is creamy. Halfway through cooking, add the fruit. Taste for salt and add as needed. When the risotto is at the correct consistency, remove from heat and stir in the remaining tablespoon of butter and the grated Parmesan.

SERVE in shallow pasta bowls topped with a sprinkling of almonds, a few mint leaves torn into fragments, and the blanched fine strips of orange zest.

VEGETABLE CRESPELLE TOPPED WITH HERB BESCIAMELLA, AL FORNO

Serves 4

Although the list of ingredients looks daunting, once the bechamel is made, it goes quickly. This herb bechamel is so good I could eat it with a spoon. The herb sprigs are removed once their flavor becomes infused into the sauce. Crespelle are the Italian version of French crepes. Crescenza is a rich and creamy, melt-in-your-mouth cheese that is worth seeking out.

FOR THE CRESPELLE
1 cup whole milk

2/3 cup unbleached, all-purpose flour

2 large eggs

Pinch of sea salt

3 tablespoons unsalted butter, plus extra for the dish

FOR THE HERB BESCIAMELLA
4 tablespoons (1/2 stick) unsalted butter

1/4 cup unbleached, all-purpose flour

2 cups whole milk

Sea salt

1 sprig fresh rosemary

1 sprig fresh sage

1 sprig fresh winter savory

1 fresh bay leaf

FOR THE FILLING
1/2 pound Swiss chard

Sea salt

2 tablespoons extra virgin olive oil

1 tablespoon diced pancetta

2 tablespoons finely diced onion

2 tablespoons finely diced carrot

2 tablespoons finely diced celery

8 tablespoons ($^1\!/_2$ cup) Crescenza cheese

$^1\!/_2$ cup freshly grated Parmigiano-Reggiano cheese

To prepare the crespelle batter, **POUR** the milk into a mixing bowl. Add the flour, shaking it through a wire strainer. Beat with a fork or a whisk until smoothly blended. Break the eggs into the bowl and add the salt. Beat thoroughly until all ingredients are well mixed. Let rest for at least 30 minutes or up to several hours.

To prepare the bechamel, **MELT** the butter in a heavy-bottomed saucepan over low heat. When the butter begins to foam, add the flour. Cook, mixing well with a wooden spoon, until golden brown. Remove from heat and let rest for 10 to 15 minutes.

While the butter-flour mixture is resting, **HEAT** the milk in another pan until it is very close to the boiling point. Put the first saucepan back over medium heat and very quickly add all of the hot milk, stirring constantly with a wooden spoon. Do not pour the milk in slowly, which can create lumps. Keep stirring, always in the same direction, again to prevent lumps from forming. Just before the sauce reaches the boiling point, add salt to taste, the herb sprigs, and the bay leaf, and continue to stir gently while the sauce cooks slowly, just below a boil, for 12 to 14 minutes, or until it resembles a thick cream. When it cools, pluck out the herbs.

To make the crespelle, **MELT** ½ teaspoon of the butter in a sauté pan over medium-low heat. As the butter melts, rotate and tilt the pan, evenly coating the bottom.

When the butter is fully melted but before it colors, **POUR** 2 tablespoons of the crespelle batter into the center of the pan. Immediately lift the pan from the burner and tip it in several directions, in a seesaw motion, to spread the batter evenly over the entire bottom of the pan.

RETURN the pan to the burner. Cook until the crespella has set and its underside has turned a light, creamy brown. Turn it over with a spatula, and brown it very lightly on the other side. Transfer it to a platter. Place wax paper between each crespella to prevent sticking. Cook the rest of the crespelle in the same manner, adding a small amount of butter, less than ½ teaspoon, to the pan before you start each one. You should have at least 8 crespelle.

To make the filling, **BLANCH** the Swiss chard in a generous amount of salted boiling water. Drain well and coarsely chop.

PREHEAT the oven to 450°F.

(continued)

HEAT the olive oil in a sauté pan over medium heat. Add the pancetta and cook for 2 minutes. Add the onion, carrot, and celery and cook for about 8 minutes, or until the onion is translucent. Add the chard and cook for 2 minutes, or until glossy. Set aside.

BUTTER the bottom of a gratin dish large enough to hold 8 rolled crespelle side by side comfortably. Spread 1 tablespoon of Crescenza along the center of one crespella. Add ¼ cup of the filling and roll like a cigar. Repeat the steps for the remaining crespelle. Arrange them in the gratin. Evenly spread about 2 tablespoons of the bechamel over the top of each crespella. Dot the surface of the crespelle with the remaining butter and sprinkle with the grated Parmesan. Bake for 10 minutes. Place under the broiler for a few minutes until the tops of the crespelle are golden brown. Let rest for a few minutes before serving.

Carefully **TRANSFER** 2 crespelle to individual serving dishes. Serve immediately.

HERB AND PARMESAN CUSTARDS WITH TRUFFLE OIL

Serves 6

This savory version of sweet custard is flavored with finely chopped herbs and Parmesan cheese. The final touches, a few drops of truffle oil over the tops and buttered, toasted crostini on the side, make this a special-occasion dish.

Unsalted butter
4 large eggs
2 cups whole milk
$^1/_2$ teaspoon finely chopped fresh rosemary
$^1/_2$ teaspoon finely chopped fresh sage
1 tablespoon finely chopped fresh flat-leaf parsley
$^1/_4$ cup freshly grated Parmigiano-Reggiano cheese
Sea salt
Truffle oil
18 thin baguette rounds, buttered and lightly toasted

PREHEAT the oven to 325°F. Butter 6 custard cups.

In a medium bowl, lightly **BEAT** the eggs with a fork. Add the milk and whisk gently to combine well. Add the rosemary, sage, parsley, and cheese. Stir until the ingredients are evenly distributed. Season with salt to taste. Divide the egg mixture among the custard cups. *(continued)*

PLACE a shallow baking pan in the oven. Arrange the prepared custard cups in the pan. Fill with enough hot tap water to come a third of the way up the sides of the custard cups.

BAKE the custards for 40 minutes, or until just firm. Remove from the water bath. Allow the custards to cool until they are tepid. Unmold onto individual serving plates. Drizzle a few drops of truffle oil over the top of each one and arrange 3 crostini on each plate.

SFORMATO OF YOUNG CAULIFLOWER AND HERB-INFUSED BESCIAMELLA

Serves 4

If you think you don't like cauliflower, tasting a small young one will convert you. It has its own special flavor and, when cooked properly, a wonderful texture. I am a big fan of cauliflower. I could eat this entire sformato myself in one sitting; it is that good.

1 pound small cauliflowers or a 1-pound cauliflower
Sea salt
2 tablespoons unsalted butter, plus extra for buttering the pan
Freshly ground black pepper
1 recipe Herb Besciamella (page 159)
4 large egg yolks
3 tablespoons freshly grated Parmigiano-Reggiano cheese
1/4 cup dried bread crumbs

PREHEAT the oven to 325°F. Bring a kettle of water to a boil.

TRIM the leaves from the cauliflowers and blanch in salted boiling water until al dente, 4 to 5 minutes. Drain well and cut into small pieces.

HEAT the butter in a medium sauté pan. Add the cauliflower and toss gently over low heat. Add salt and pepper to taste. Sauté for 4 to 5 minutes to flavor the cauliflower.

STIR the cooled bechamel, eggs, and Parmesan together in a large bowl using a wooden spoon. Add the cauliflower, season with salt and pepper to taste, and gently mix all the ingredients together. *(continued)*

BUTTER a standard loaf pan and coat it with the bread crumbs, tapping out the excess. Pour the cauliflower mixture into the pan. Place a roasting pan in the oven. Fill with enough hot water to come a third of the way up the sides of the loaf pan. Carefully set the loaf pan in the hot water bath.

BAKE the sformato for 1 hour, or until just firm. Remove from the water bath and cool until tepid. Unmold the sformato onto a serving platter and serve immediately.

SFORMATO OF GREEN CAULIFLOWER AND GOAT CHEESE

Serves 4

Romanesco broccoli, a type of green cauliflower, is a delicate, delicious vegetable with a startling green color. It is combined with the lemony tang of goat cheese in this sformato, or unmolded savory "pudding."

> 4 large eggs, lightly beaten with a fork
> 1 pound whole-milk ricotta
> $^1/_2$ pound goat cheese
> 4 tablespoons extra virgin olive oil
> 2 garlic cloves, finely chopped
> 3 tablespoons chopped fresh flat-leaf parsley
> 1 pound Romanesco broccoli, white cauliflower, or Broccoflower, cored and cut into
>   small pieces
> Sea salt
> Unsalted butter
> Dried bread crumbs

PREHEAT the oven to 375°F.

In a large bowl, **COMBINE** the eggs, ricotta, and goat cheese. Stir until well mixed. Set aside.

In a large sauté pan, **WARM** the olive oil. Add the garlic and parsley and sauté over low heat for about 5 minutes. Add the cauliflower pieces and stir well to coat them. Add ½ to 1 cup water and salt to taste. Cook until the cauliflower is tender but not soft and the water evaporates. Let cool for a few minutes. *(continued)*

ADD the cauliflower mixture to the cheese and eggs. Stir together gently with a wooden spoon. Add salt to taste.

Generously **BUTTER** a loaf pan and coat heavily with bread crumbs, tapping out the excess. Transfer the mixture to the prepared pan. Bake for about 1 hour, or until light golden on top. Remove from the oven and let settle for about 10 minutes. Carefully unmold onto a serving dish.

WARM LAMON BEANS WITH GRILLED RADICCHIO

Serves 4

Dried Lamon beans have a rich, nutty-sweet flavor, just like the fresh ones. The skin of both fresh and dried turns a warm earth brown when cooked.

   1¹/₂ cups dried Lamon (borlotti) or pinto beans
   Extra virgin olive oil
   Sea salt
   4 heads radicchio
   Freshly ground black pepper

SOAK the beans overnight in enough water to very generously cover them. Drain.

PLACE the beans in a soup pot and add water to cover generously. Bring to a boil. Cover and simmer over very low heat until the beans and skin are tender. Time varies according to the "freshness" of the dried beans. Check after 1 hour and continue cooking as long as needed until the beans are tender.

When the beans are tender, **DRAIN.** Coarsely mash them with a wooden spoon, adding enough olive oil to form a coarse puree. Add salt to taste and keep warm while you grill the radicchio.

HEAT an outdoor grill or turn on the broiler.

(continued)

CUT the radicchio heads in half lengthwise. Brush the surfaces with olive oil. Grill or broil until the radicchio is tender, sprinkling with salt to taste. Use tongs to turn the radicchio several times. Grill for about 6 minutes, or until a thin wooden skewer inserted into the base meets with a little resistance and the leaves are wilted.

To serve, **MOUND** the bean puree on a serving dish and place the grilled radicchio next to it. Drizzle both with additional olive oil and grind black pepper over the top.

CIMA DI RAPA WITH BLACK OLIVES AND FRESH BAY LEAVES

Serves 4

I prefer to think of this category of green vegetable—often termed bitter greens—as pungent or tonic greens. They have powerful beneficial properties. For some, greens are an acquired taste. But I grew up eating wild mustard greens and have always loved the flavor. *Cima di rapa*, broccoli rabe, has that same exciting quality.

Fresh bay leaves have amazing aromatic qualities dramatically different from musty dried leaves in jars. Grow European bay in a pot on the back steps, on a terrace, or in the garden as a tree. I have a large tree in my garden and a pot growing close by the kitchen for easy access when I'm cooking.

$^1/_4$ cup extra virgin olive oil
3 garlic cloves, coarsely chopped
4 fresh bay leaves, torn in half
$1^1/_2$ pounds broccoli rabe, stems trimmed
Sea salt
$^1/_4$ cup oil-cured black olives, pitted and halved
4 thick lemon wedges
Grilled rustic bread

PLACE the olive oil, garlic, and bay leaves in a large sauté pan. Sauté over low heat until the garlic is translucent, about 4 minutes.

CUT the broccoli rabe and tender stems crosswise into 3-inch lengths. Add to the sauté pan along with 1 cup water and salt to taste, and stir. Raise the heat to medium; when the water comes to a boil, lower the heat to low. Add the olives and stir. Cook until the greens are tender, another 8 to 10 minutes. Taste for salt. Serve with lemon wedges and grilled bread on the side.

BAKED CHICKPEAS IN BUTTER WITH ROSEMARY SPRIGS

Serves 4 to 6

Chickpeas are transformed when sautéed in butter instead of the traditional olive oil. Rosemary lends a deep, resinous herbal note to the dish.

  1 pound dried chickpeas, soaked overnight in water to generously cover,
      drained, and rinsed
  Sea salt
  4 or 5 sprigs fresh rosemary
  3 large garlic cloves, lightly crushed
  Pinch of hot red pepper flakes
  Freshly ground black pepper
  4 tablespoons ($^1/_2$ stick) unsalted butter

PREHEAT the oven to 350°F.

PLACE the chickpeas in a large, deep, glazed terra-cotta braising pan or, second best but still perfectly fine, a heavy-bottomed metal braising pan. Add water to cover generously and a pinch of salt. Add 2 sprigs of the rosemary, the garlic, red pepper, and a few coarse grindings of black pepper.

COVER the pan and place it in the oven. Bake until the chickpeas are tender. Time will vary according to how old the chickpeas are, but count on at least 1 hour or maybe even 2. Check the water level every so often, adding hot water as needed to cook the chickpeas completely. A couple of inches of flavorful broth should remain when they are done. Also check for salt, adding it as needed while the chickpeas bake.

MELT the butter in a large sauté pan. Add 2 or 3 rosemary sprigs. Add 2 cups of the chickpeas. (Use the remaining chickpeas in other recipes in the book.) Sauté over low heat, stirring to coat the beans and letting the rosemary become fragrant.

BROCCOLI RABE IN LEMON CREAM

Serves 4

Pungent greens are usually paired with olive oil, and that is how I often cook them. I thought it might be interesting to soften the bitterness by using cream and brighten up the flavor with a touch of lemon. I was very pleasantly surprised by the results—an unexpectedly delicious dish.

    1$^1/_2$ pounds broccoli rabe, stems trimmed, cut into short lengths
    Sea salt
    3 tablespoons unsalted butter
    $^1/_4$ cup heavy cream
    1 teaspoon lemon juice
    Buttered crostini

COOK the broccoli rabe in abundant salted boiling water until al dente, about 8 minutes. Drain.

MELT the butter in a large sauté pan. Add the rabe and stir well to coat. Add salt to taste and let the flavors meld over low heat for about 5 minutes.

ADD the cream and lemon juice. Toss gently and let warm over low heat. Serve surrounded with crisp buttered crostini.

WHOLE ESCAROLE STUFFED WITH CURRANTS, SUN-DRIED TOMATOES, AND TOASTED PINE NUTS

Serves 4

In the past, escarole was one of the few tangy greens found in the market, perhaps because it is one of the mildest in flavor. Escarole unfolds in the garden like a ruffled rose, green outer leaves with a pale yellow heart. Darker leaves are great for cooking; lighter leaves go into salads. Plucked from the garden, the entire vegetable is tender enough to eat raw.

Here, whole braised escarole becomes a bundle filled with tasty morsels.

1 large head escarole
3 tablespoons extra virgin olive oil, plus extra for drizzling
1 heaping tablespoon pine nuts, lightly toasted
1 tablespoon currants
2 tablespoons Sun-dried Tomatoes (page 63), drained
2¹/₂ cups dry white wine
Sea salt

OPEN up the escarole like a flower. Drizzle with the 3 tablespoons olive oil. Evenly distribute the pine nuts, currants, and tomatoes amid the escarole leaves. Re-form the escarole, cradling the leaves together securely. Tie the escarole with a string to maintain its shape and keep the stuffing ingredients inside.

BRING the wine, 5 cups of water, and salt to taste to a gentle simmer in a large saucepan. Carefully submerge the stuffed escarole in the liquid. Place a small plate on top of the escarole to keep it submerged while cooking. Simmer, uncovered, until tender, about 10 minutes.

(continued)

Gently **LIFT** the escarole out of the liquid with a large slotted spoon, letting the excess liquid drain away.

PLACE on a cutting board and cut into 4 wedges. Serve drizzled with a touch of olive oil.

PUGLIESE CATALOGNA CHICORY WITH RED ONION AND SALAME

Serves 4

I discovered this long-leafed green chicory during my summers spent in a small town on the coast of Puglia. Preparing this dish from the tender leaves I grow brings back a flood of memories.

> ¼ cup extra virgin olive oil
> 3 whole garlic cloves
> Pinch of hot red pepper flakes
> ½ red onion, thickly sliced
> About 1 pound Pugliese Catalogna chicory or dandelion greens, cut into short lengths
> Sea salt
> ¼ cup slivered Italian salame

HEAT the olive oil in a large sauté pan. Add the garlic, red pepper, and onion. Sauté over low heat until the onion is tender, about 10 minutes.

STIR in the chicory, salt to taste, and ½ cup water. Cook until the chicory is tender and the water is evaporated. Add the salame a few minutes before the chicory is done, and let it warm through. Serve warm or at room temperature.

PIZZA WITH POTATO AND ARUGULA

Makes 4 individual pizzas

Yukon gold potatoes are most similar to the variety I cooked with during my summers in the Salento. The butter-yellow color and superb flavor of the potatoes create a golden, crusty topping. Sprinkle the raw arugula over the top for a peppery finish.

Pizza Dough (page 58)
1¼ pounds potatoes, preferably Yukon gold
6 tablespoons extra virgin olive oil
Sea salt
2 garlic cloves, mashed to a paste in a mortar and pestle
Hot red pepper flakes
Freshly grated pecorino cheese
Handful of arugula leaves, cut into strips

PREPARE the pizza dough as directed and let it rest. Place a baking stone on the top oven rack and preheat the oven to 350°F.

Meanwhile, **PEEL** and thinly slice the potatoes. Place in a bowl and toss with 2 table-spoons of the olive oil. Arrange the potato slices on a baking sheet in a single layer. Bake until they begin to color lightly, about 15 minutes, turning the slices over halfway through cooking. Remove the potatoes from the oven and, using a spatula, carefully transfer them to a platter. Sprinkle with salt to taste.

In a small bowl, **COMBINE** the remaining 4 tablespoons olive oil and the garlic.

RAISE the oven temperature to 500°F. (The baking stone should heat for at least 30 minutes.) Shape the pizzas according to the directions on page 57. Brush the surface of each pizza with a little of the olive oil and garlic mixture, and sprinkle with red pepper. Arrange the potatoes over the top in an overlapping pattern. Brush the remaining oil and garlic mixture over the top and sprinkle with pecorino.

BAKE the pizzas until the potatoes and crust are golden, 6 to 8 minutes. Remove from the oven and scatter arugula leaves over the top.

PANINI WITH GREENS, BLACK OLIVES, AND RICOTTA

Makes 4 panini

I've always found the combination of greens, black olives, and fresh ricotta to be perfection. And grilled panini are so quick to make. Before you know it, a satisfying hot meal awaits.

About $^3/_4$ pound assorted greens, sweet and bitter, such as romaine,
    endive, and broccoli rabe
Sea salt
$^3/_4$ pound whole-milk ricotta, well drained
Freshly ground black pepper
2 tablespoons extra virgin olive oil, plus extra for drizzling
1 large garlic clove, finely chopped
$^1/_8$ teaspoon hot red pepper flakes
$^1/_4$ cup pitted, coarsely chopped oil-cured black olives
4 squares purchased high-quality focaccia

STRIP away any coarse stems and finely chop the greens.

PLACE about ½ cup water in a medium sauté pan. Add the greens and sprinkle with a pinch of salt. Cook over medium heat, stirring once or twice, for 4 to 5 minutes, or until tender. Check to make sure the water does not completely evaporate and, if necessary, add a little more water. Drain well in a colander and gently press out excess water with the back of a wooden spoon.

PLACE the ricotta in a small bowl. Season with salt and black pepper to taste; set aside. Heat a stove-top grill or light the broiler.

PLACE the olive oil, garlic, and red pepper in a medium sauté pan. Cook over low heat for 2 to 3 minutes. Add the greens and olives and stir to combine. Cook over medium-low heat for about 5 minutes, stirring occasionally, until excess moisture evaporates.

Meanwhile, **SPLIT** the focaccia in half horizontally. Lightly grill the focaccia halves cut side down, or toast them, cut side up, under the broiler. Drizzle the cut sides with olive oil. Place a layer of the greens on the bottom halves of the bread. Top with ricotta. Cover with the top halves of the bread. Place in a panini machine or a 450°F oven until the focaccia is hot and crusty. Serve warm.

GREEN OLIVE AND MEYER LEMON RELISH

Serves 4

Meyer lemons, fully ripened to a rich golden yellow and fresh off the tree, are incredibly tender and sweet. Here, I use the entire lemon, including the peel, pith, and flesh. Although the pith is commonly thought to be bitter, it is, in fact, sweet, and has an interesting soft texture I find very appealing. In addition, it is a repository for a concentrated amount of vitamins and minerals. Crisp, fleshy green olives are important in this relish. I've discovered one that I think works well here—the Baresane olive. But any fleshy, crisp green olive can be used.

The relish can be used as a spread on panini, served as a topping for grilled fish, or tossed with diced, cooked potatoes or cooked rice for a refreshing potato or rice salad. Simply increase the amount of olive oil accordingly.

1 cup medium to large green olives, such as Baresane, in brine, drained
2 large Meyer lemons
1 to 2 teaspoons home-dried Italian oregano (page 64)
3 tablespoons extra virgin olive oil
Sea salt
Freshly ground black pepper

USE a paring knife to slice thick strips of olive flesh from the pits.

CUT the lemons into ¼-inch slices. Stack several slices at a time and carefully cut into small dice.

COMBINE the olives and lemons in a bowl. Sprinkle with oregano to taste. Add the olive oil and salt and pepper to taste. Stir gently to combine ingredients.

SERVE the relish immediately or let it rest in a cool place for about an hour to allow flavors to mingle.

RED CARROTS SOTT'ACETO WITH HOT RED PEPPERS

Makes 1 pint

Most people think of pickling vegetables as a labor-intensive process that requires waiting for months before being able to enjoy the end result. These stunning strips of red carrots in wine vinegar and piquant seasonings mellow overnight, turning a deep garnet color. The pickled carrots are ready to eat the next day.

Serve as a garnish to grilled panini or as part of an antipasti platter.

4 medium red or orange carrots
2 tablespoons extra virgin olive oil
2 sprigs fresh oregano
1 large garlic clove, cut in half
2 small fresh hot red peppers
Sea salt
Best-quality red wine vinegar

BRING a pot of salted water to a boil. Trim and peel the carrots. Cut into ¼-inch-thick batons 2 inches long. Blanch for 2 minutes. Drain immediately and let dry well on paper towels.

PLACE the carrots in a glass jar with a screw-top lid. Add the olive oil, oregano sprigs, garlic, whole peppers, and salt to taste.

COVER generously with vinegar. Screw the cap on the jar and refrigerate for 24 hours. Remove the carrots from the marinade and store in a glass jar. If left too long, they become too sharply acidic. Serve cold or at room temperature.

RED WINE SCIROPPO

Makes about 1¹/2 cups

This full-bodied sweet red wine syrup (*sciroppo*) will surprise you. It has a diverse array of ingredients that merge to taste unlike anything I have ever made. Again, I look to the garden for the bay leaves and the lemon rind, important flavorings, to which I add a split vanilla bean and peeled chestnuts.

Though it's delicious on vanilla custard (page 185) or ice cream, I can't resist dipping my finger in the syrup for a little taste just on its own. The syrup is also delicious over baked pears.

1 bottle rich red wine, preferably Italian
¹/₂ cup sugar
2 large fresh bay leaves, torn in half
Long, wide ribbon of Meyer lemon zest
1 vanilla bean, split lengthwise
4 or 5 peeled chestnuts

COMBINE all the ingredients in a heavy-bottomed medium saucepan. Stir well and bring the wine to a boil. Simmer, uncovered, over medium heat until reduced to about 1½ cups. It should not be too thick, but a dense liquidy syrup.

STRAIN out the solids. Store the syrup in a glass jar in the refrigerator.

EAT the chestnuts separately or chop them and use to top vanilla ice cream.

VANILLA CUSTARD WITH RED WINE SCIROPPO

Serves 6

Simple homemade custard is one of my favorite comfort desserts. Since it is winter, I drizzle the custards with a deep ruby-colored syrup made from reduced red wine and flavorings.

> Unsalted butter
> 4 large eggs
> ½ cup sugar
> 2 cups whole milk
> 1 teaspoon vanilla extract
> Pinch of sea salt
> Red Wine Sciroppo (page 184)

BUTTER six ½-cup custard cups and set aside. Preheat the oven to 325°F and bring a kettle of water to a boil.

In a medium bowl, lightly **BEAT** the eggs with a fork. Add the sugar, milk, vanilla, and salt. Whisk gently until well incorporated.

POUR the custard mixture into the custard cups. Place a roasting pan in the oven. Arrange the custard cups in the pan. Fill with enough hot tap water to come a third of the way up the sides of the custard cups.

BAKE for 40 minutes, or until just firm. Carefully remove the cups from the water bath.

SERVE slightly warm, or refrigerate and serve lightly chilled. Just before serving, drizzle with Red Wine Sciroppo.

BITTER ORANGE GELATO WITH MINT LEAVES

Makes 1 pint

Since my neighborhood climate is mild, and hot days are few and far between, oranges do grow but they never become really sweet. My next-door neighbor's tree bears an enormous amount of fruit, most of which ends up on the grass to be gathered and tossed out with the garden trimming.

I like the somewhat acidic edge their oranges have and my neighbors are happy to offer them to me. I use the juice in place of lemon or vinegar in salad dressings and in numerous other ways. The aromatic peel creates a slightly tart, refreshing gelato, but any organic orange peel can be used. Just reduce the sugar by 1 or 2 tablespoons.

> 2 cups whole milk
> 1/2 cup sugar
> Zest of 1 large orange (use a vegetable peeler to remove only
>   the outer orange skin, not the pith)
> 4 large egg yolks
> Sprigs fresh mint

PLACE the milk, ¼ cup of the sugar, and the orange zest in a saucepan and bring to a boil. Remove from heat. Cover and set aside until the milk is strongly perfumed with orange, about 30 minutes or up to an hour. Check occasionally until the orange presence is strong but not overpowering. Remember that when frozen, the flavor will lose some of its intensity.

In a medium bowl, **WHISK** together the remaining ¼ cup sugar and the egg yolks until the mixture thickens and turns pale yellow.

STRAIN the milk mixture into a medium bowl to remove the orange peel, letting as much milk as possible drain from the peel. Measure the milk and add more if needed to make 2 cups.

PLACE the milk in a saucepan and bring to a boil. Remove from the heat and slowly whisk half the milk into the egg and sugar mixture. Whisk in the remaining milk.

POUR the milk-egg mixture back ino the saucepan and place over medium heat. Using a wooden spoon, stir constantly until the mixture is thick enough to coat the back of the spoon. Pour into a bowl and keep stirring until the mixture cools.

FREEZE in an ice-cream machine following the manufacturer's directions.

To serve, **SCOOP** the gelato into chilled metal or glass goblets. Press a mint sprig in the center of each serving.

SPRING

THE FIRST SIGN OF SPRING came very early. A pot of grape hyacinths bloomed and faded, came and went. I saw them but could not believe it possible that spring was actually on its way. It creeps in little by little. A wild seed blows in on a breeze and blooms unexpectedly with small coral flowers. Arugula from last season sends up new leaves between the stones, and so do the dandelions that grow wild. Climbing roses show delicate new fans of reddish leaves and pink blossoms.

A borage plant, another seed from last year's garden, grows and grows into a magnificent *cespuglio,* a bush, bearing periwinkle-colored, star-shaped flowers and masses of leaves, gifts from the warm awakening earth. I clear away the deadwood of winter. I am on vigilant watch for slugs and snails, which I feel guilty about destroying, but what can I do if I cultivate an organic garden? I work the earth here and there, dense from pounding, persistent rain, to find worms squirming and wiggling, surprised by the intrusion. They are my friends. They aerate the soil and help bring plants up toward the sun.

The citronella and hydrangeas appear to be dead from afar. But closely scrutinizing the branches and twigs, I start to see movement, infinitesimal green leaflets. My fig tree, all winter long an attractive skeleton, starts to push a green bud out here, another out there. Then, in mere days, large leaves unfurl.

The citrus trees—two Meyer lemons and a Persian lime—are green-leafed all year round. Now they are fringed with tender sprays of russet leaves that hold the promise of more green foliage ahead. At the same time, plump, golden fruits dangle on the stems among the glossy leaves.

Hollyhocks—old-fashioned fig-leafed plants in peach, white, and aubergine—

grow six feet tall and sway in a spring breeze. Rust has invaded the lovely leaves. I know the air in San Francisco is too moist. I'll have to say a sad good-bye to them.

Among the herbs, rosemary, that stalwart evergreen, is dense with deep blue blossoms. Winter savory, pruned down to woody twigs, is a mass of tender pungent leaves. Italian oregano grows tall on either side of the path between the two olive trees. When the wind whips up, the olive leaves flicker pewter and green.

Other volunteers in the garden are nasturtiums, real charmers. Water lily–shaped leaves and flower buds grow in long trailing garlands. The flowers and leaves are both edible, related to watercress. The petals—orange, saffron, rouge, and creamy yellow—open their faces to the sun. Thick clumps of plump chives are adorned with spiky lavender flowers that surprise with a softness to the touch when they first bloom.

Artichoke plants, all eight of them, have grown four feet tall. Even without the edible bud, they would be striking in any garden landscape with their impressive long, silvery gray serrated leaves. Already they have put out their first little bud that never gets larger and looks like a little ornament on top of a Christmas tree. But now the plants have moved on to produce the large central bulbs with baby artichokes on either side. This garden vegetable is so lovely I hesitate to harvest it. But that long, tasty stem, that big, tightly closed *carciofo*, begs to be cooked and savored.

I bend down to smell and touch other aromatic plants. They transport me to the Mediterranean, to the *scogliera*, the cliffs overlooking that transcendent sea. Silver and green santolina, lacy artemisia, woodsy thyme—these tough, resilient plants withstand far harsher conditions than in my temperate garden.

Geraniums, so integral to the Italian garden and a flower I especially prize, have just burst into full bloom. They are all in pots since they grow best in tight boots. I daily deadhead the spent blossoms of rose, white blushed with pink, and deep magenta, and remove any yellowing leaves to promote growth and protect the plant from rot, a pleasant chore for me.

The *Washingtonia robusta*, Mexican fan palm, grows taller each year. Someday it might reach a whopping one hundred feet. Right now it is about six feet tall. The accordion-like leaves fringed with thin, brown fibers gleam in the new sun.

Three tall cypresses set the tone and give structure to my Italian garden. I am grateful they survive the wet, gusty winters and keep growing taller and bushier. All too often I have seen cypresses in San Francisco suffer instant death, overnight turning brown from head to toe from too much water. I never water them. The box hedges, also important structural statements, are glossy and splendid, neat, symmetrical green partitions that create rooms within the long expanse of the garden.

Soeur Agnes (Sister Agnes) white oleanders are vigorous growers. Right now their leaves are tipped with unopened buds. Yes, they are poisonous, but so are a multitude of plants in the garden. No self-respecting Italian garden can be without them. The Mediterranean colors—Turkish red, peach gelato, limestone yellow—are a reflection of that land of sun and heat.

My poor bougainvillea struggles, but I won't give up. Surprisingly, these plants grow with wild abandon in San Francisco even though we have no real summer and just a few truly hot days annually. No Italian nights of heat and humidity; instead, fog and wind. Still, they flourish and bloom extravagantly. Mine is still a pathetic sculpture of sticks this year. Although bougainvilleas are very slow to grow in general, I gave this one a poor start by planting it in the wrong spot initially. Now it has all the right conditions. But since the bougainvillea hates being transplanted, it is giving me a hard time. I'll feed it, examine its dry branches very closely. I'll praise it and apologize to it for uprooting it. Hopefully, it will forgive me and gift me with an abundance of brilliant fuchsia against a hot stone wall, where it most certainly has found a home.

It's time to bring out the cushion for the wrought-iron chaise and lie in the mild sun, perhaps with a light blanket over me. But this is also the time to put in seeds, plant, hoe, feed, rake.

Although I try to lounge and luxuriate in the elixir of spring scents, I am up and down constantly, performing garden tasks small and large. How to enjoy my Italian garden and let work wait until tomorrow?

PIATTI FORTI · *Main Dishes*

Crespelle Filled with Sautéed Lettuces and Ricotta Topped with Crisped Prosciutto   220

Frittata with Tender Radish Leaves   222

Thin Parmesan Frittata Topped with Fresh Field Salad   224

Fresh Borlotti Bean Puree with Sautéed Catalogna Chicory   226

Artichokes, Wild Spring Greens, and Yellow Potato Stufato   228

VERDURE · *Vegetables*

Fresh Peas with Wild Fennel and Hot Red Pepper   229

Red Carrots with Honey and Balsamic Vinegar   230

Spinach Sautéed with Spring Herbs   231

Fresh Fava Beans with Parsley, Mint, Marjoram, and Thyme   232

Mustard Greens all'Aglio   233

Whole Braised Young Fennel with Hot Red Pepper and Extra Virgin Olive Oil   234

PIZZA AND PANINI

Pizza Topped with Fresh Ricotta and Arugula   235

Pizza Verde with Artichoke Hearts and Herbs   236

Panino with Mozzarella and Parsley and Almond Relish   237

CONDIMENTI · *Condiments*

Meyer Lemon Marmellata   238

Parsley and Almond Relish   240

DESSERTS

Fragole di Bosco with Sugar and Lemon   241

Ricotta with Citrus Zest and Rum   242

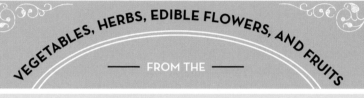

· Spring Garden ·

Alloro · European bay

Bietola di Chioggia · Chioggia beets

Borragine · borage

Carciofi · artichokes

Carota Nantese di Chioggia · Chioggia carrots

Cicoria Catalogna Pugliese · long-leafed chicory

Erba cipollina · chives

Erbette · cut-and-come-again ribless chard

Fagioli borlotti lingua di fuoco · climbing borlotti beans

Fagioli rampicante Lamon · climbing Lamon (borlotti) beans

Fave · fava beans

Finocchio · bulb fennel

Finocchio selvatico · wild fennel

Fragola di bosco · tiny wild strawberries

Lattugha Romana · romaine lettuce

Maggiorana gentile · sweet marjoram

Menta · mint

Misticanza quattro stagioni · four-season mixed chicories and lettuces

Origano · Italian oregano

Piselli · peas

Prezzemolo gigante di Napoli · large flat-leaf Neapolitan parsley

Ravanelli · radishes

Rosmarino · rosemary

Rucola selvatica · wild arugula

Satureja montana · winter savory

Soncino · mâche

Spinaci · spinach

BURRATA WITH GARNISHES

Serves 4

Burrata is an exquisite fresh cheese once made from buffalo milk. As with many southern Italian fresh cheeses, such as mozzarella, cow's milk is now used. *Burrata* is the Italian word for buttered, and one taste of its soft crust enclosing a delectable creamy but light cheese will make you an *appassionato*, a passionate fan. It is one of the finest soft, fresh cheeses I've ever tasted.

A few crisp and aromatic edible garnishes allow the cheese to be enjoyed in *purezza*, in its pure state, while adding just the right touch of contrasting textures and colors from the garden. Remember to harvest radishes as soon as they begin to rise to the surface of the soil. Otherwise, they turn too peppery and the flesh becomes spongy instead of crisp and juicy.

> 12 fresh-pulled young radishes with leaves
> 1 pound burrata cheese
> Extra virgin olive oil
> Handful of wild or cultivated arugula leaves

Out in the garden, **PLACE** the radishes in a large colander and spray with the garden hose to wash away garden soil. Inside the kitchen, soak the radishes in a bowl of cool water and gently agitate them to help dislodge the soil. Lift the radishes out of the water to avoid disturbing any dirt that has settled in the bottom of the bowl. Clean the bowl and repeat the process until no soil remains in the bowl. Remove any large, wilted, or yellowed leaves from the radishes. Let the radishes dry on kitchen towels.

SLICE the cheese lengthwise into 4 equal pieces. Place 1 slice on each serving plate. Drizzle the burrata with olive oil. Garnish with little bouquets of whole radishes and arugula leaves. Serve with crusty bread.

PINZIMONIO

Pinzimonio is simply dipping the very first and most tender vegetable of each season into highly flavorful olive oil and seasoning it with a touch of salt. Pinzimonio can be a selection of several seasonal new raw vegetables. But offering only one raw vegetable, such as exquisite baby artichokes, captures the true essence of the pinzimonio experience.

The very first of the new artichokes, only about 2 inches long, are so tender that very little trimming is required. Rub the exterior of the artichokes with lemon to avoid discoloration.

Baby artichokes
Extra virgin olive oil
Sea salt

ARRANGE the artichokes on a platter. Place a small bowl of olive oil and a saucer of salt on the table. Each person dips the artichoke in the olive oil, sprinkles it with sea salt, and nibbles away at the tiny, tender vegetable.

FRESH-PULLED RADISHES STUFFED WITH GREEN OLIVE BUTTER

Serves 4

Radishes are one of the most rewarding crops to grow, since they mature in the blink of an eye. Just be sure not to leave them in the ground for too long or they will turn pungent. Pull them out as soon as they pop their little heads out of the soil.

For this recipe, the radishes are simply split lengthwise, tender leaves and all. One half is spread with green olive butter and then sandwiched together with the other half to look like a whole, fresh-picked radish.

I've discovered a delicious, crisp olive, the Baresane, that has all the right qualities for this preparation. If unavailable, many other varieties are in the marketplace waiting to be discovered.

12 fresh-pulled young radishes with leaves

4 tablespoons (¹/₂ stick) unsalted butter, at room temperature

¹/₄ cup pitted, finely chopped crisp green olives

Out in the garden, **PLACE** the radishes in a large colander and spray with the garden hose to wash away garden soil.

Inside the kitchen, **PLUCK** off any wilted yellow leaves. Immerse in a large bowl of cold water and agitate to loosen the remaining soil. Let sit for several minutes. Carefully lift the radishes out of the water to avoid disturbing any dirt that has settled in the bottom of the bowl. Repeat several times until no soil or grit remains in the water. Let the radishes dry on kitchen towels.

Meanwhile, **PLACE** the butter and olives in a small bowl and mash with a fork until well combined.

(continued)

SPLIT the radishes lengthwise through the leafy tops. Spoon a teaspoon of the olive butter on one half of the radish and sandwich together with the other half.

PLACE in the refrigerator briefly to firm up the butter. Serve at room temperature as an antipasto accompanied by a clean and bright-tasting cold white wine.

ERBETTE BUNDLES

Serves 6

Erbette leaves make wonderful wrappers for any number of fillings. Creamy Crescenza, a member of the Stracchino family of cheeses, creates a melt-in-your-mouth filling.

> Sea salt
> 6 large erbette leaves or green leaves of Swiss chard
> 1/2 cup Crescenza cheese
> 1/2 cup whole-milk ricotta
> Extra virgin olive oil

PREHEAT the oven to 350°F. Bring a large pot of salted water to a boil.

IMMERSE each leaf, one at a time, in boiling water until it is bright green and fully tender, 4 to 5 minutes. Carefully lift each leaf out of the water without tearing the leaves. Lay them out flat on a work surface and pat dry with a clean dishtowel.

In a small bowl, **MASH** together the Crescenza and ricotta. Place a heaping tablespoon of the cheese mixture along one long edge of each leaf. Roll the leaf around the cheese mixture to form a cigar shape. Fold the edges over to seal in the cheese mixture.

MOISTEN the exterior of the rolls with olive oil and season lightly with salt. Arrange the rolls on a baking dish and place in the oven for about 5 minutes, or until the leaves are warm to the touch and the cheese is just melted.

REMOVE from the oven and transfer to a serving platter. Drizzle with olive oil and serve immediately.

WARM AVOCADOS ON THE HALF-SHELL

Serves 4

I grew up in Southern California, avocado country, and have been an ardent fan since childhood. Here, pitted, unpeeled avocado halves are warmed in the oven, filled with chive-and-Meyer-lemon-zest butter, and garnished with chive blossoms.

Although avocados are still considered a bit exotic in Italy, they are imported and appear in markets. And while chives too are still a bit of a novelty for Italian cooks, they lend an additional level of sophistication to this dish, as does the dollop of caviar topping each avocado.

Chives do not respond well to the marketplace. By the time they reach your kitchen, they've become stringy and limp. Freshly cut, chives are plump, succulent, tender, and highly aromatic. Growing your own gives you a new appreciation of this delicate member of the onion family. It had that effect on me. Another bonus is the edible blossoms, a mauve shade, with which to garnish this dish.

A reminder about edible flowers: They are not just lovely plate decorations but contain vitamins, minerals, and all kinds of as yet unclassified substances that work in synergy to enhance our health.

2 large Hass avocados, ripe but firm (the flesh should be green throughout with no blemishes or bruises)
$^1/_2$ Meyer lemon and 1 teaspoon grated zest
5 tablespoons unsalted butter, at room temperature
2 tablespoons finely cut chives (use kitchen shears)
Sea salt
Best-quality caviar, about 2 ounces
Tender, small chive blossoms

PREHEAT the oven to 325°F.

Carefully **CUT** the avocados in half without removing the peel. Gently twist to separate the halves. Insert a sharp paring knife in the pit and lift it out. Immediately squeeze lemon juice over the exposed avocado flesh.

PLACE the avocados on a baking sheet, cut side up. If necessary, cut a small slice off the bottom of each avocado to stabilize it. Warm the avocados in the oven for 5 to 7 minutes. Be sure to remove them when just warmed through, since too much heat will compromise the flavor and texture.

Meanwhile, **MASH** together the butter, chives, and lemon zest. Do this just before serving; otherwise the chive flavor tends to become too dominant.

SPRINKLE with sea salt and arrange the avocados on individual serving plates. Spoon a generous tablespoon of chive butter in the center of each avocado and top with a generous spoonful of caviar. Garnish with chive blossoms.

MISTICANZA SALAD

Serves 4

The Italian version of the French mesclun, *misticanza* is a mix of very young leaves of various chicories and sweet lettuces.

My cut-and-come-again mix of salad greens has been providing me with *misticanza* salads for a year from the original planting of seeds, thanks to the cool conditions in the garden. Gather the leaves when still small, or simply cut off the entire tender head, leaving the base of the plant still in the ground; it will produce another head.

My mix has quite a few different chicories, each unique in appearance. Nasturtiums, those indefatigable garden flowers, have made their way into the *misticanza* patch, contributing garlands of beautiful flowers and saucer-shaped leaves that also find their way into my salads.

If the *misticanza* is too pungent for your palate, add a handful of mint leaves to sweeten the salad.

About 4 cups different varieties of small chicory leaves
3 to 4 tablespoons extra virgin olive oil
3 to 4 tablespoons best-quality red wine vinegar
Sea salt
Fresh mint leaves (optional)

WASH the chicory well in a bowl of water, lifting out the greens and repeating in several changes of water until no soil remains at the bottom of the bowl. Air-dry on kitchen towels.

PLACE the whole leaves in a shallow salad bowl. Dress with olive oil, vinegar, and salt. Taste and correct the seasonings. Tangy greens require more olive oil and vinegar than do sweet-leafed lettuces. If desired, add mint leaves and toss again.

SPRING CAPRESE

Serves 4

This take on the classic summer *caprese* uses the fresh, light flavor and moist texture of mozzarella slices in combination with some of spring's tenderest offerings—young, sweet radishes, the tiniest fava beans, "green" almonds, and a sprinkle of chives to announce the end of winter and herald the arrival of spring.

Springtime almonds are milky white, crisp, and juicy. The shells are green and fuzzy, not yet turned hard and brown. If impossible to find, substitute almonds soaked in cool water for one hour. Peel and split the almonds lengthwise.

Four 4-ounce fresh mozzarella balls, brought to room temperature
Sea salt
$1/4$ cup extra virgin olive oil, plus extra for drizzling
16 fresh-pulled young radishes with leaves, washed and quartered
    lengthwise (page 197)
Handful of tender radish leaves, slivered
$1/2$ cup shelled young fava beans, unpeeled
$1/2$ cup almonds (see headnote), split in half
3 tablespoons snipped fresh chives
Nasturtium blossoms

SLICE the mozzarella into rounds. If very moist, drain on kitchen towels.

ARRANGE the mozzarella in a slightly overlapping pattern on a large serving dish. Season with salt. Drizzle with ¼ cup olive oil.

Evenly DISTRIBUTE the radishes, radish leaves, fava beans, and almonds over the cheese. Drizzle with olive oil as desired and season with salt to taste. Sprinkle with chives and garnish with nasturtium blossoms.

INSALATA DI CAMPO

Serves 4

A salad of true wild field greens gathered in nature is as delicious and healthful as any dish I can think of. During stays in Italy I have had many opportunities to gather the greens myself and prepare salads from whatever was emerging from the earth.

My garden offers a similar experience, since I made sure to plant cultivated varieties of many of the greens that grow spontaneously in Italian soil. And far from being bothered, I'm delighted when wild dandelions appear in the garden. The leaves, when picked young, add a great tangy touch.

When leaves are small, always serve them whole to maximize their vitality. When greens are cut, they lose precious minerals and vitamins.

Handful of tender small assorted chicory leaves
Handful of young romaine leaves
Handful of arugula leaves
Handful of very young dandelion greens
Handful of small nasturtium leaves
Handful of small mint leaves
Extra virgin olive oil
Red wine vinegar
Sea salt

WASH the tender leaves carefully so as not to bruise them. Do not tear or chop the leaves. Air-dry on kitchen towels. Place the leaves in a shallow salad bowl and toss with your hands to mix the different leaves. Season with olive oil, vinegar, and salt. Toss briefly and serve immediately.

SONCINO WITH MIMOSA DRESSING

Serves 4

Lamb's lettuce, called *soncino* in Italy and various other names depending on the region, is perhaps more commonly known here by its French name, *mâche*. A delicate, spoon-shaped green leaf, it is sweet and succulent. If you haven't tasted it, you will surely fall in love with this lovely springtime lettuce. Finely sieved hard-cooked egg yolks give the appearance of fuzzy mimosa blossoms, which bloom in the spring. Together, the lettuce and eggs create a charming salad of beauty and substance.

4 handfuls mâche or butter lettuce leaves, carefully washed and air-dried on kitchen towels
$^1\!/_4$ cup extra virgin olive oil
2 teaspoons red wine vinegar
3 hard-cooked large eggs, peeled and yolks finely sieved
Sea salt
Freshly ground black pepper

PLACE the lettuce in a shallow salad bowl. Drizzle with olive oil and vinegar. Carefully toss just once or twice since the delicate leaves wilt or bruise easily.

SPRINKLE the sieved egg yolks over the top and season with a little salt and pepper. Serve immediately.

LEEK SOUP WITH BASIL TOPPING

Serves 4 to 6

Pull up some leeks from the garden, and gather some greens. Substance comes from the slice of country bread placed at the bottom of each bowl, with the soup ladled over the top. A final sprinkling of basil perfumes the soup.

$1/4$ cup extra virgin olive oil

3 medium leeks, trimmed, white and light green parts thinly sliced

Handful of dandelion greens, finely sliced

Leaves from 1 bunch beets, stems cut away, coarsely chopped

Sea salt

Freshly ground black pepper

4 to 6 slices country bread, toasted

$1/4$ cup slivered fresh basil

HEAT the olive oil in a soup pot. Add the leeks and cook over medium heat, stirring frequently, until the leeks begin to wilt. Add the dandelion and beet greens and lightly sauté for 1 to 2 minutes. Add $1\frac{1}{2}$ quarts water and bring the soup to a boil. Cook over medium heat until the greens are tender. Add salt and pepper to taste.

PLACE a slice of toasted bread in each bowl. Ladle the soup over the top and sprinkle with basil. Serve immediately.

RICE, FAVA BEAN, AND SPRING GREENS SOUP

Serves 4

When the fava bean plants were tall and leafy and bearing exquisite pale lavender and white miniature blossoms, I was excitedly waiting for the first fava bean pod to appear. Each day I would hunt through the dense clusters of tender leaves but find no trace of a pod.

Then, I looked again among the leaves, and, almost overnight, fava bean pods small and sweet-looking were everywhere, hidden among the foliage that is the exact same shade of green. It is at this point that the race begins, since the fava bean plant produces and produces.

Coinciding with the appearance of the fava beans are borage and other greens that rise to bask in the warm sun. For this soup I assembled a bit of all the new greens and the first of the fava beans to celebrate the turning of the seasons.

$1/4$ cup extra virgin olive oil, plus extra for drizzling
1 spring onion, finely chopped
Handful of tender dandelion greens, finely slivered
Handful of small borage leaves, coarsely chopped
Sea salt
$1/2$ cup Arborio rice
1 cup shelled young fava beans, unpeeled
$1/2$ teaspoon chopped fresh marjoram
$1/4$ cup slivered fresh basil, cut at the last moment

PLACE the olive oil and onion in a soup pot. Cook over low heat until the onion wilts, about 6 minutes.

ADD the dandelion greens and borage to the soup pot and add salt to taste. Stir for several minutes to let the flavors develop.

ADD 2 quarts water to the pot and bring to a boil. Simmer until the greens start to become tender, about 10 minutes.

ADD the rice and cook at a low simmer, stirring frequently, for about 8 minutes. Stir in the fava beans and simmer another 4 minutes, or until the rice is cooked but just slightly al dente.

REMOVE from heat, sprinkle in the marjoram and basil, and stir. Ladle into individual shallow soup bowls and drizzle with a touch of olive oil.

ZUPPA DI LATTUGHA

Serves 2

This soup has a gentle rather than strong flavor. A small amount of broth concentrates the sweet, delicate nature of romaine from the garden.

    6 small heads romaine lettuce
    Sea salt
    1 garlic clove, cut in half
    Cubes of day-old rustic bread
    Extra virgin olive oil
    Freshly grated Parmesan cheese
    Freshly ground black pepper

Gently **TEAR** the romaine leaves into medium-sized pieces. In a medium soup pot, combine the romaine and 1½ cups water. Add salt to taste. Simmer until the lettuce is tender, about 5 minutes.

Meanwhile, lightly **RUB** the cut side of the garlic clove on all sides of the bread cubes and place in shallow soup bowls. Drizzle the bread with olive oil. Ladle the romaine and juices over the bread. Drizzle again with olive oil, sprinkle with Parmesan, and coarsely grind a bit of pepper over the top.

DITALINI WITH FRESH PEAS, GRATED PECORINO, AND HOME-DRIED ITALIAN OREGANO

Serves 4 to 6

Dried oregano with sweet peas from the garden may seen an unusual pairing, but this rustic dish hits all the right notes.

Italian oregano is highly perfumed, not harsh, which may explain the success of this dish.

1 pound imported ditalini
Sea salt
$\frac{1}{4}$ cup extra virgin olive oil
2 garlic cloves, finely chopped
About 2 cups shelled fresh peas
Home-dried Italian oregano (page 64)
Freshly grated pecorino cheese

COOK the pasta in abundant boiling salted water until al dente.

Meanwhile, **PLACE** the olive oil and garlic in a large sauté pan. Sauté gently over low heat for 2 to 3 minutes.

ADD the peas, oregano, salt to taste, and water to cover. Bring to a gentle boil. Simmer until the peas are tender, 5 to 6 minutes.

DRAIN the pasta and add to the sauté pan. Stir for several minutes over low heat to let the pasta absorb flavor. Serve sprinkled with pecorino.

SPAGHETTINI WITH WILD FENNEL, HOT RED PEPPER, AND CRUNCHY BREAD TOPPING

Serves 4

This is a take on the classic Sicilian *pasta con sarde*. Pasta with fresh sardines, wild fennel, pine nuts, not-too-sweet raisins, and saffron may sound bizarre, but when made with fresh and authentic ingredients, it is considered one of the great pasta dishes in all of Italy.

I use the sweet licorice-flavored tender feathery tops of the wild fennel I grow in my garden from seed, add a touch of hot red pepper to bring it in balance, and finish it with a topping of toasted bread crumbs, used instead of grated cheese on various pastas from southern Italy.

2 cups chopped wild fennel tops, tender stems and feathery parts only
Sea salt
Pinch of saffron threads
6 tablespoons extra virgin olive oil, plus 2 teaspoons for bread crumbs
1 garlic clove, finely chopped
$^1/_8$ teaspoon hot red pepper flakes
1 pound imported spaghettini
$^3/_4$ cup bread crumbs, toasted

COOK the fennel greens in abundant salted boiling water until tender, about 15 minutes. Remove the greens with a slotted spoon, reserving the cooking water. Crumble the saffron into ½ cup of the reserved water. Set aside.

Finely **CHOP** the fennel. Set aside.

COMBINE the 6 tablespoons olive oil, the garlic, and the red pepper in a large sauté pan. Cook over low heat until the garlic is soft and fragrant. Add the fennel to the pan and stir well, fluffing up the chopped fronds to break up any clumps. Add the ½ cup reserved water with saffron and let simmer gently for 10 minutes to blend flavors.

SAUTÉ the bread crumbs in the remaining 2 teaspoons olive oil over medium heat until crisp and golden. Set aside.

Meanwhile, **BRING** the remaining fennel cooking water to a boil, adding extra water if needed for the pasta. Cook the pasta until al dente. Drain, reserving some of the broth. Toss the pasta with the fennel sauce and add some of the cooking liquid to create a small amount of broth.

SERVE with toasted bread crumbs on the side for each person to sprinkle over the pasta.

PASTA TOSSED WITH RICOTTA AND ERBETTE

Serves 4 to 6

I can never get enough erbette, a ribless small-leafed Swiss chard. Its flavor is gentle yet full of pleasing mineral taste, and it cooks quickly. It has a place in every cook's garden. Ricotta, mild and sweet, adds substance without overpowering the greens.

Sea salt
3 tablespoons extra virgin olive oil
2 tablespoons unsalted butter
1 large garlic clove, crushed
4 cups torn erbette leaves or green leaves of Swiss chard
1 pound imported egg fettuccine
1/4 pound whole-milk ricotta, at room temperature
Freshly grated Parmesan cheese

BRING a large pot of salted water to a boil. Place the olive oil, butter, and garlic in a large sauté pan. Cook slowly until the garlic releases its scent, about 4 minutes. Add the greens, 1 cup water, and salt to taste. Cook until tender, about 5 minutes.

Meanwhile, COOK the fettuccine. Drain when al dente. Gently toss the pasta with the greens and ricotta. Serve topped with Parmesan.

PASTA WITH FAVA BEANS, PARSLEY, BUTTER, AND BLACK PEPPER

Serves 4 to 6

A big bunch of flat-leaf parsley from the garden sautéed with garlic makes a wonderful pasta sauce on its own. Since the fava beans are so abundant, I've added them—always delicious with pasta.

> 1 pound imported penne rigate
> Sea salt
> 3 tablespoons unsalted butter
> 1/4 cup chopped fresh flat-leaf parsley
> 3 garlic cloves, coarsely chopped
> 2 cups shelled young fava beans, unpeeled
> Extra virgin olive oil
> Freshly ground black pepper

COOK the pasta in abundant boiling salted water until al dente.

Meanwhile, in a large sauté pan, **COMBINE** the butter, parsley, and garlic. Cook over low heat until the garlic is tender, about 3 minutes.

ADD the fava beans, 1 cup water, and salt to taste. Simmer until the beans are tender, about 6 minutes.

DRAIN the pasta and toss with the sauce and juices. Distribute among pasta bowls, drizzle with olive oil, and top with a grinding of black pepper.

RISOTTO WITH BORAGE LEAVES, CARROT SLIVERS, AND PANCETTA

Serves 4

From one or two original plants grown from seed, many more borage plants pop up as the wind blows. I cook only the tender leaves. Larger leaves become coarse and prickly.

The starry blue flowers look lovely, taste lightly of cucumber, and can be scattered over salads or used as a garnish for cool drinks such as iced tea or lemonade.

 4 cups young borage leaves, about 3 inches long
 Sea salt
 2 tablespoons extra virgin olive oil
 1 small onion, finely diced
 2 garlic cloves, finely chopped
 3 tablespoons chopped pancetta
 2 cups Arborio rice
 6 cups vegetable or meat broth, brought to a simmer
 $\frac{1}{4}$ cup slivered carrots
 2 tablespoons unsalted butter
 About $\frac{1}{2}$ cup freshly grated Parmesan cheese
 Freshly ground black pepper

COOK the borage in abundant boiling salted water until tender. Cooking time will vary depending on the tenderness of the leaves, from 10 to 30 minutes. Drain, coarsely chop the leaves, and set aside.

In a deep, heavy-bottomed saucepan, **COMBINE** the olive oil, onion, garlic, and pancetta. Sauté over low heat until the onion is translucent, about 10 minutes. Add the rice and stir until the grains are coated with the mixture, 2 to 3 minutes. Stir in the borage.

ADD enough broth to just cover the rice and vegetable mixture. Bring to a gentle simmer. Stir until the liquid is absorbed. Continue in this way until the rice is cooked through but slightly al dente. During the final additions of broth, add the carrot slivers and cook until tender.

REMOVE from heat and add the butter and Parmesan. Top with pepper. Serve in shallow bowls.

DOUBLE FENNEL RISOTTO

Serves 4

The licorice taste of bulb fennel is strongest when just harvested. This is the point at which it is full of sweet juices. These start to evaporate as the fennel travels to market, dissipating the taste and making the fennel fibers tough.

Wild fennel grown from seed or collected in nature adds extra licorice flavor and some deep green color to the dish. How nice to grow it in the cool spring garden and enjoy all it has to offer.

2 tablespoons extra virgin olive oil

3 tablespoons unsalted butter

$\frac{1}{2}$ onion, finely diced

4 small fennel bulbs or 2 larger ones, trimmed lightly and cut into small dice

3 tablespoons chopped fresh flat-leaf parsley

3 tablespoons chopped wild fennel tops

Sea salt

2 cups Arborio rice

6 cups vegetable or meat broth, brought to a simmer

5 tablespoons freshly grated Parmesan cheese

Freshly ground black pepper

PLACE the olive oil, 2 tablespoons of the butter, and the onion in a heavy-bottomed saucepan. Cook over low heat until the onion is translucent, about 10 minutes.

ADD the diced fennel, parsley, fennel tops, and salt to taste. Sauté for 5 minutes. Add the rice to the fennel mixture and stir to coat the grains completely. Add enough broth to just cover the ingredients.

RAISE the heat slightly and continue to cook, stirring, until the liquid is absorbed. Repeat until all the broth has been absorbed, or until the rice is tender, with a little bite, and the risotto is still moist.

REMOVE from heat and stir in the remaining 1 tablespoon butter, the Parmesan, and pepper to taste.

CRESPELLE FILLED WITH SAUTÉED LETTUCES AND RICOTTA TOPPED WITH CRISPED PROSCIUTTO

Serves 4

Crespelle, Italian for crepes, are good wrappers for a myriad of fillings. They are a quick and delightful way to prepare a version of cannelloni.

With so many varieties of lettuces and chicories in my garden, I've picked a basketful to prepare the filling.

Strips of crisped prosciutto make a fine crunch as a topping.

1 recipe crespelle (page 159)
4 cups chopped assorted garden greens such as chicories, lettuces,
    nasturtium leaves, and borage
Sea salt
1 cup whole-milk ricotta, at room temperature
1 large egg, lightly beaten
$\frac{1}{2}$ cup freshly grated Parmesan cheese, plus extra for sprinkling
Freshly ground black pepper
Unsalted butter
3 to 4 thin slices prosciutto, cut diagonally into long strips

PREPARE the crespelle according to the directions on page 160. Preheat the oven to 400°F.

Meanwhile, **COOK** the greens, uncovered, in just enough water to cover them, adding salt to taste. When tender, drain excess water. Chop the greens.

In a bowl, **STIR** together the greens, ricotta, egg, Parmesan, and salt and pepper to taste.

PLACE a large spoonful of the mixture along one side of each crespelle, mounding the mixture gently. Roll the crespelle into cylinders.

BUTTER a baking dish just large enough to contain the crespelle in one layer. Arrange the crespelle in the dish. Top with a little thinly sliced butter and a sprinkling of Parmesan.

BAKE, uncovered, until hot all the way through and lightly brown on top, about 15 minutes.

Meanwhile, **CRISP** the prosciutto strips in a hot sauté pan and set aside.

LET the crespelle rest briefly. Scatter with the prosciutto and serve.

FRITTATA WITH TENDER RADISH LEAVES

Serves 4

Spring, and I was lunching at an outdoor caffè in the Villa Borghese, the magnificent park perched atop the historical heart of Rome. My mixed salad contained, among other leafy greens, tender radish leaves. When I remarked how tasty they were, my *cameriere* (server) informed me that Romans like to sauté the radish leaves in garlic to make into a frittata. *Eccola!* Here is the recipe.

Sea salt
2 cups tender radish leaves, coarsely chopped
5 tablespoons extra virgin olive oil
2 garlic cloves, finely chopped
6 to 8 large eggs
3 tablespoons freshly grated pecorino Romano cheese
Freshly ground black pepper

PREHEAT the broiler.

POUR water 2 inches deep in a large sauté pan. Bring to a boil and add salt. Add the radish leaves and cook for 5 minutes, or until tender. Drain well.

In a sauté pan, **COMBINE** 3 tablespoons of the olive oil and the garlic. Sauté for 2 to 3 minutes over low heat. Add the radish leaves and salt to taste. Continue cooking over low heat for another 2 to 3 minutes, or until the leaves have absorbed the flavor of the olive oil and garlic.

BREAK the eggs into a bowl and beat lightly with a fork. Add the radish leaves, pecorino, and salt and pepper to taste, and gently beat with a fork. Heat the remaining 2 tablespoons olive oil in a medium skillet, tilting the pan to coat the bottom and sides. When the oil is hot, add the egg mixture. Lower the heat and cook slowly, stirring frequently, until the eggs have formed small curds but the top is still runny.

To cook the top, **PLACE** the pan under the broiler (or in a preheated 400°F oven) until the frittata browns very lightly and the top is firm. Check often, since overcooking the frittata will toughen it. Remove the pan from the heat and let rest briefly. Place a plate over the top of the pan and invert the frittata onto it.

SERVE the frittata at room temperature, cut into wedges.

THIN PARMESAN FRITTATA TOPPED WITH FRESH FIELD SALAD

Serves 4

Here, a very thin frittata serves as a base for a topping of *insalata di campo*, a field salad. This makes a wonderful lunch or brunch dish, simple to prepare and lovely to look at.

6 large eggs
2 garlic cloves, finely chopped
3 tablespoons freshly grated Parmesan cheese, plus extra for sprinkling
Sea salt
Freshly ground black pepper
Extra virgin olive oil
Insalata di Campo (page 205)

BREAK the eggs into a bowl and beat them lightly with a fork. Add the garlic, Parmesan, and salt and pepper to taste.

PLACE enough olive oil in a large sauté pan to lightly coat the bottom; turn the heat to medium. Pour a ladleful (about a quarter) of the egg mixture into the pan and swirl it around just as you would when making a crepe. Lower the heat to medium-low. When the frittata turns opaque, carefully flip it over and lightly cook the other side. Repeat, making 4 thin, crepelike frittatas.

To serve, **TOP** each frittata with Insalata di Campo and a sprinkling of grated Parmesan.

FRESH BORLOTTI BEAN PUREE WITH SAUTÉED CATALOGNA CHICORY

Serves 4

This is a complete meal that is deeply satisfying. Cooking fresh borlotti beans changes their brilliant cream and burgundy speckled color to earthy brown, but the flavor is exceptional. The mineral-rich chicory is equally robust.

With garlic-rubbed bread, one can't ask for a more fulfilling eating experience.

$^1/_4$ cup extra virgin olive oil, plus extra for drizzling

1 tablespoon chopped fresh winter savory or thyme

2 garlic cloves, coarsely chopped

2 cups cooked fresh borlotti beans, put through a food mill

Sea salt

1 pound Catalogna chicory or dandelion greens

HEAT 2 tablespoons of the olive oil in a sauté pan. Add the savory and half the garlic and cook for 2 minutes, or until fragrant. Add the beans and stir for 2 minutes, or until hot. Transfer to a plate and set aside.

BRING 1 cup salted water to a boil in a large pot. Boil the chicory until tender, about 10 minutes. Drain.

SAUTÉ the remaining olive oil and garlic until fragrant. Add the chicory and stir until glossy, about 4 minutes.

PLACE the chicory on one side of a plate and the beans on the other. Drizzle with olive oil.

ARTICHOKES, WILD SPRING GREENS, AND YELLOW POTATO STUFATO

Serves 4

With my artichoke plants, I can produce many dishes—actually, an endless variety. This stew combines wedges of artichokes and diced new potatoes with a few wild green offerings from the garden.

> 4 medium artichokes, trimmed lightly, each cut into 8 wedges, kept in acidulated water
> 6 tablespoons extra virgin olive oil, plus extra for drizzling
> 2 garlic cloves, coarsely chopped
> Sea salt
> 2 cups coarsely chopped assorted greens such as arugula, dandelion greens, chicories, and borage leaves
> 6 small Yukon gold potatoes, boiled until tender but firm, drained

DRAIN the artichokes well. Place in a braising pan with the olive oil, garlic, and salt to taste. Cook slowly over low heat until tender, about 8 minutes.

ADD the greens and water to cover; simmer until tender.

STIR in the potatoes gently so as not to crush them. Warm them in the mixture for a few minutes to allow them to absorb the flavors. If the stew becomes too dry, add water. There should be a small amount of broth. Check for salt since potatoes require enough salt to counter their mild taste. Divide the stew among shallow bowls and drizzle with olive oil.

FRESH PEAS WITH WILD FENNEL AND HOT RED PEPPER

Serves 4

This was served to me by a friend in Puglia—all harvested from his organic *orto* (vegetable garden). It is a surprising blend of sweet peas and a touch of licorice from the wild fennel, the sweetness brought to earth by the bite of hot red pepper.

1 medium onion, finely chopped

1 tablespoon finely diced pancetta

3 tablespoons extra virgin olive oil

Pinch of hot red pepper flakes

2 pounds unshelled fresh peas, shelled to yield about $^3/_4$ pound

6 generous sprigs young wild fennel, tender stems and feathery parts only

Sea salt

Freshly ground black pepper

COOK the onion and pancetta in the olive oil in a small braising pan over medium-low heat until the onion is tender and the pancetta has rendered the fat, 10 to 12 minutes. Add the red pepper.

STIR in the peas and fennel sprigs. Cook for 3 or 4 minutes. Add 1 cup water and a pinch of salt. Cover the pot and simmer for about 15 minutes, or until the juices have reduced to a small amount of liquid. Taste and season with additional salt and pepper as needed.

RED CARROTS WITH HONEY AND BALSAMIC VINEGAR

Serves 4

This amazing combination of flavors can be used as a vegetable side dish or condiment. Red carrots are not an uncommon sight in Italy. Carrots of any color, all in a row, look lovely growing in the garden with their fine leafy tops—which are also edible, cooked in soups or vegetable stews.

> 1 pound red or orange carrots, peeled and cut into batons
> Sea salt
> 1/4 cup extra virgin olive oil
> 1/4 cup best-quality balsamic vinegar
> 2 tablespoons honey
> 3 sprigs fresh thyme

COOK the carrots in heavily salted water until al dente. Drain.

PLACE the olive oil, vinegar, honey, thyme, and ½ cup water in a saucepan and bring to a simmer. Lower the heat, add the carrots, and simmer for about 15 minutes, or until the carrots are tender but firm. Stir to keep coating the carrots with the juices.

SERVE warm or at room temperature.

SPINACH SAUTÉED WITH SPRING HERBS

Serves 4

When picked young, spinach does not have a chance to develop a heavy presence of oxalic acid. Cooked with a bouquet of fresh spring herbs, the dish turns out beautifully green and sweet.

$1/4$ cup extra virgin olive oil
$1/2$ cup tender nasturtium leaves (no larger than 2 to 3 inches), stemmed
$1/4$ cup slivered young mint leaves
3 tablespoons finely snipped fresh chives
1 garlic clove, coarsely chopped
4 cups very young spinach, leaves no more than 3 inches long, well washed
Sea salt

HEAT the olive oil in a large sauté pan over low heat. Toss in the nasturtium, mint, chives, and garlic and cook until fragrant. Toss in the spinach and salt to taste. Cook, stirring, until tender, about 5 minutes.

FRESH FAVA BEANS WITH PARSLEY, MINT, MARJORAM, AND THYME

Serves 4

I've always been enamored of fava beans—so sweet and vegetal, with a pleasing note of bitterness. They can be cooked simply in olive oil, but with a garden full of fresh herbs at the ready, the fava beans become heady with mingled perfumes.

3 tablespoons extra virgin olive oil, plus extra for drizzling
2 garlic cloves, finely chopped
$^1/_2$ cup chopped mixed fresh herbs, primarily flat-leaf parsley with hints of mint, marjoram, and thyme
2 cups shelled young fava beans, unpeeled
Sea salt

PLACE the olive oil in a large sauté pan. Add the garlic and herbs. Warm over low heat.

ADD the fava beans, salt to taste, and 1 cup water. Stir and simmer until the beans are tender. Remove from heat and drizzle with a little more olive oil. Serve hot or warm.

MUSTARD GREENS ALL'AGLIO

Serves 4 to 6

Even as a child, I loved the bracing taste of pungent greens and would drink the cooking liquid, which my little body must have instinctively known was healthful.

Pungent greens, wild or cultivated, are one of the secrets of good health. Not a day goes by In Italy without at least one plate of greens appearing on the dining table.

> 2 pounds mustard greens
> Sea salt
> $^1/_2$ cup high-quality red wine vinegar
> 3 garlic cloves, thinly sliced
> Generous handful of small mint leaves (about 16)
> $^1/_2$ cup extra virgin olive oil

STRIP the coarse ribs from the mustard greens. Cook the leaves in abundant boiling salted water until tender, about 8 minutes, or longer depending on size and freshness.

Meanwhile, in a small saucepan, BRING the vinegar and garlic to a gentle boil. Cook until the liquid is reduced to a quarter of its original volume, about 8 minutes.

DRAIN the greens well, pressing out excess moisture with the back of a wooden spoon. Place on a platter and fluff up the leaves with a fork. Tear the mint leaves and sprinkle them over the greens. Cover to keep warm.

POUR the reduced vinegar, including the garlic, over the mustard greens and mint. Drizzle with the olive oil and salt to taste. Toss until the leaves are glossy. Taste and add more oil if desired. I always finish this dish with a generous drizzle of olive oil before serving. Serve warm or at room temperature.

WHOLE BRAISED YOUNG FENNEL WITH HOT RED PEPPER AND EXTRA VIRGIN OLIVE OIL

Serves 4

Fennel can be eaten raw, grilled, and sautéed, but braising really brings out a richness that is incomparable. Garden bulb fennel, young, tender, and juicy, melts in your mouth in this memorable preparation.

1/4 cup extra virgin olive oil
1 teaspoon hot red pepper flakes or 1 dried hot red pepper, crumbled
8 baby fennel bulbs, trimmed lightly
1/2 cup dry white wine

PLACE the olive oil, red pepper, and fennel in a braising pan over medium heat. Cook for 15 minutes, stirring every 2 minutes. The fennel may get a little golden around the edges, which adds to the flavor. Add ¼ cup water and the wine and cook, covered, until tender, about 15 minutes.

PIZZA TOPPED WITH FRESH RICOTTA AND ARUGULA

Makes 4 individual pizzas

Mild ricotta is sweet and light, a good contrast to the deliciously peppery wild arugula.

Pizza Dough (page 58)
Extra virgin olive oil
Sea salt
3/4 pound whole-milk ricotta, at room temperature
Big handful of wild arugula leaves

When the 4 balls of dough have rested for about half an hour, **PLACE** a baking stone on the top rack of the oven and turn the heat to 500°F. Let the stone heat for at least 30 minutes.

SHAPE the pizzas according to the directions on page 57.

DRIZZLE the pizza with olive oil, sprinkle with sea salt, and slide it onto the baking stone in the oven. Bake until the edges are golden, 6 to 8 minutes, and remove from the oven.

Immediately **SPREAD** the pizza with a quarter of the ricotta, drizzle with olive oil, sprinkle with sea salt, and tent with aluminum foil to keep warm. Repeat with the remaining pizzas. After all the pizzas have been baked, scatter each pizza with arugula leaves and serve immediately.

PIZZA VERDE WITH ARTICHOKE HEARTS AND HERBS

Makes 4 individual pizzas

I saw this particular pizza years ago in a shop window in Italy and was impressed by its "greenness." It's a wonderful pizza for springtime, when artichokes are incredibly good and herbs are abundant and tender.

Pizza Dough (page 58)
3 tablespoons extra virgin olive oil
3 garlic cloves, finely chopped
$1/4$ cup chopped fresh flat-leaf parsley
2 tablespoons chopped fresh mint
4 artichokes, lightly trimmed and cut into thin slivers, kept in acidulated water
Sea salt

When the 4 balls of dough have rested for about half an hour, **PLACE** a baking stone on the top rack of the oven and turn the heat to 500°F. Let the stone heat for at least 30 minutes.

Meanwhile, in a large sauté pan, **COMBINE** the olive oil, garlic, parsley, and mint. Stir over low heat until the parsley is tender and bright green.

DRAIN the artichoke slivers and add to the pan, along with salt to taste. Sauté over medium heat until the artichokes are tender but hold their shape. Set aside.

SHAPE the pizzas according to the directions on page 57. Spread a quarter of the artichoke and herb mixture on each pizza and slide it onto the baking stone in the oven. Bake until the edges are golden, 6 to 8 minutes. Remove from the oven and serve immediately.

PANINO WITH MOZZARELLA AND PARSLEY AND ALMOND RELISH

Makes 1 panino

A panino is a great treat for lunch or a picnic. The parsley and almond spread makes a tasty addition to the mild, sweet flavor of moist mozzarella.

Always use the best country-style bread you can find.

1 fresh mozzarella ball, about 8 ounces
2 slices country bread
Parsley and Almond Relish (page 240)

SLICE the mozzarella about ¼ inch thick. If very moist, drain on a kitchen towel. Layer the cheese on one slice of bread. Spread with a generous amount of the relish. Cover with the remaining slice of bread. Eat right away or wrap well and eat within an hour or so.

MEYER LEMON MARMELLATA

Makes about 4 cups

My garden's Meyer lemon trees are my pride and joy. They are a continual source of delight all year round—glossy green leaves, intensely fragrant blossoms, and glorious deep gold sweet citrus fruit. Once established, a Meyer lemon tree will reward you with a tremendous yield of fruit in a continuous cycle.

> 10 large Meyer lemons
> Sugar

USE a paring knife to carefully cut the zest from 8 lemons. Slice the zest into ⅛-inch strips and put in a medium bowl. Reserve the remaining 2 lemons for juice.

With a paring knife, **QUARTER** the 8 lemons and remove any seeds. Coarsely chop the lemon pulp and pith and measure the resulting amount. Add an equal amount of water. Pour the lemon pulp and water mixture into the bowl with the zest and stir. Set aside for at least 4 hours at room temperature or refrigerate, covered, overnight.

POUR the mixture into a heavy-bottomed braising pan. Add the same amount of sugar as you did water in the preceding step. Juice the remaining 2 lemons and add to the pan.

STIR and bring to a boil over medium-high heat. Let cook, uncovered, at a steady simmer for 30 minutes, or until the mixture thickens to a dense syrup. Ladle the marmalade evenly into four 1-cup jars with screw tops and let cool, uncapped. Screw on the caps and refrigerate. The marmalade will thicken further as it chills.

If you like to can jams and produce, **PACK** the marmalade into sterilized jars and follow your method for canning, in which case the marmalade can be stored in the pantry and will not require refrigeration until opened.

PARSLEY AND ALMOND RELISH

Makes ³/4 cup

The bracing quality of raw flat-leaf parsley is a powerhouse flavor enhancer. I've added chopped almonds and salt-cured nasturtium buds and bound it with olive oil, lemon juice, and lemon zest.

This makes a wonderful spread on panini, a topping for fresh mozzarella, or, with additional olive oil, a raw sauce for freshly cooked hot pasta—the heat of the pasta releases the perfumes and lightly "cooks" the parsley.

1 bunch fresh flat-leaf parsley, stems removed (about 2 cups loosely packed)
¹/4 cup almonds, toasted (see page 29) and chopped
2 tablespoons Salt-cured Nasturtium Buds (page 66) or salt-cured capers
¹/4 cup extra virgin olive oil
3 tablespoons Meyer lemon juice
Zest of ¹/2 Meyer lemon
Sea salt

CHOP the parsley finely and place in a bowl. Add the almonds and nasturtium buds and stir to combine.

In a small bowl, **COMBINE** the olive oil, lemon juice, zest, and salt to taste. Beat lightly with a fork for a moment. Set aside to let the flavors develop.

Immediately before using, **STIR** together the parsley mixture and the dressing. Leftover relish may lose some of its brilliant green color because of the lemon juice, but the flavor will still be good.

FRAGOLE DI BOSCO WITH SUGAR AND LEMON

Serves 2 to 3

They're not big, and not really juicy, but wild strawberries, *fragole di bosco*, are very special indeed and can be cultivated in the garden. This runnerless strawberry is a pretty plant that produces tiny, tasty, highly perfumed fruits. Since the strawberries are so small, it is worthwhile to plant generously.

Fragile to the extreme, wild strawberries are a gardener's treat that travel directly to the kitchen to be eaten right away. If you have just a few, sprinkle the strawberries over Meyer Lemon Gelato or panna cotta (pages 69 and 130).

1 pint wild or other small, ripe strawberries
Sugar
A few drops of Meyer lemon juice

WIPE the strawberries clean with a damp paper towel. Spread the fruit on a plate. Sprinkle with sugar to taste and a few drops of lemon juice. Do not stir. Serve right away.

RICOTTA WITH CITRUS ZEST AND RUM

Serves 2

In this simple but refined dessert, the tender, highly perfumed lemon zest deeply imbues the ricotta with the flavor and fragrance of lemon. The most aromatic oils from the lemon peel begin to lose strength a mere thirty minutes after picking the fruit. But don't give up if you only have supermarket lemons. This will still be a lovely spring dessert. Just make sure the lemons are organic.

$1/2$ pound whole-milk ricotta

2 tablespoons sugar

$1/2$ teaspoon rum

1 teaspoon grated Meyer or organic market lemon zest

12 whole almonds, toasted (page 29)

PLACE the ricotta in a bowl and beat with a whisk. Add the sugar, rum, and lemon zest. Stir well with a wooden spoon until smooth. Cover the bowl and refrigerate for about an hour to allow flavors to mellow.

REMOVE the ricotta from the refrigerator and bring to room temperature.

Thinly **SLIVER** the almonds. Transfer the ricotta to a serving platter and form into a mound. Cover with the almonds. Serve immediately.

SOURCES FOR ITALIAN SEED VARIETALS

I use Franchi seeds almost exclusively in my garden with great success. Below are sources for Franchi seeds as well as other companies that carry Italian varietals.

Cook's Garden
P.O. Box C5030
Warminster, PA 18974
(800) 457-9703
www.cooksgarden.com

Daylight Farms (heirloom Italian seeds
from Franchi Sementi by mail)
850 North Cabrillo Highway
Half Moon Bay, CA 94019
(650) 726-4980
daylightfarms@aol.com
www.farmerjohnspumpkins.com

Fratelli Ingegnoli
(English catalogue available)
Via O Salomone 65
20138 Milano, Italy
www.ingegnoli.it

Johnny's Selected Seeds
955 Benton Avenue
Winslow, ME 94901
(877) 564-6697
www.johnnyseeds.com

Pagano Seeds
c/o Lake Valley Seeds
5717 Arapaho Street
Boulder, CO 80303
(303) 449-4882
www.lakevalleyseed.com

Renee's Garden
7389 West Zayante Road
Felton, CA 95018
(888) 880-7228
www.reneesgarden.com

Seeds from Italy (Franchi Sementi seeds
available on the Internet)
P.O. Box 149
Winchester, MA 01890
(781) 721-5904
seeds@growitalian.com or
bmckay@growitalian.com
seedsfromitaly.com

Well-Sweep Herb Farm
205 Mt. Bethel Road
Port Murray, NJ 07865
(908) 852-5390
www.wellsweep.com

INDEX

Almonds
  avocado on the half-shell with, 34
  dried fig and toasted almond "pesto," 125
  my ricotta dessert, 68
  parsley and almond relish, 240; panino with, 237
  ricotta with citrus zest and rum, 242
  risotto with green tomatoes and, 106–7
  spring caprese salad, 204
  toasted, radicchio di Castelfranco with warm butter and, 91
  zucchini carpaccio with, 29
Anchovies
  orecchiette with cima di rapa and hot red pepper, 103
  potato and escarole salad with, 147
  risotto verde, 44
  truffled anchovy butter: fettuccine with tomato and, 154–55; warm crostini topped with crispy sage leaves and, 141–42
Antipasti: fall, 81–87; spring, 195–201; summer, 19–27; winter, 139–42. See also Salad(s)
  Adriatic figs stuffed with stracchino cheese, 81
  autumn antipasto basket, 82
  bresaola involtini, 84
  burrata with garnishes, 195
  ceci crisped in hot herbed extra virgin olive oil, 139
  erbette bundles, 199
  fresh-pulled radishes stuffed with green olive butter, 197–98
  fresh ricotta with basil and parsley, 19
  hard-cooked eggs wrapped in giant basil leaves, 26–27
  La Baronessa's roses, 20–21
  pinzimonio, 196
  ricotta and caprino layered with fresh basil leaves, 24–25
  sun-dried Principe Borghese tomatoes wrapped in capocollo salame, 140
  tiny herb frittatas, 22–23
  warm avocados on the half-shell, 200–201
  warm crostini topped with Dolcelatte Gorgonzola butter, 87
  warm crostini topped with truffled anchovy butter and crispy sage leaves, 141–42
  whole sage leaves in pastella, 85–86
Artichokes, 6, 74–75, 189
  artichoke and leek risotto with cream, 110–11
  artichokes, wild spring greens, and yellow potato stufato, 228
  pinzimonio, 196
  pizza verde with artichoke hearts and herbs, 236
  young, pasta with parsley, white wine, and, 104
Arugula, 134, 188
  artichokes, wild spring greens, and yellow potato stufato, 228
  bresaola involtini, 84
  burrata with garnishes, 195
  insalata di campo, 205
  pasta with almost every herb in the garden, 41–42
  Pino's pizza, 57–58
  pizza topped with fresh ricotta and, 235
  pizza with potato and, 178–79
Autumn antipasto basket, 82
Avocados
  avocado on the half-shell, 34
  warm avocados on the half-shell, 200–201

Balsamic vinegar, red carrots with honey and, 230
Barley soup with summer herbs, 36
Basil, 6, 14, 20, 37. *See also* Herbs
    avocado on the half-shell, 34
    fresh ricotta with parsley and, 19
    green beans with European-style butter and basil
      leaves, 52
    hard-cooked eggs wrapped in giant basil leaves,
      26–27
    La Baronessa's roses, 20–21
    leek soup with basil topping, 207
    panini with grilled zucchini, ricotta salata, and, 62
    pastas with: spaghettini with basil leaves and
      strands of lemon zest, 37; spaghetti with tomato
      sauce and fresh basil leaves, 38; tubetti la favorita,
      40
    rice, fava bean, and spring greens soup, 208–9
    ricotta and caprino layered with fresh basil leaves,
      24–25
    Sicilian zucchini al picchi pacchi with, 54
    soup with new potatoes, saffron, mascarpone, and,
      35
Bay, 131, 171
    cima di rapa with black olives and fresh bay leaves,
      171
    red wine sciroppo, 184
    young fennel with bay leaves and garlic, 119
Beans
    borlotti: assorted green chicory soup with pancetta
      and, 100; fresh borlotti bean puree with sautéed
      Catalogna chicory, 226–27
    fava: fresh, with parsley, mint, marjoram, and
      thyme, 232; pasta with parsley, butter, black
      pepper, and, 215; rice, fava bean, and spring
      greens soup, 208–9; spring caprese salad, 204
    green beans with European-style butter and basil
      leaves, 52
    Lamon beans: Lamon bean salad, 146; warm, with
      grilled radicchio, 169–70
    passato of cannellini beans and cima di rapa, 151
Bechamel. *See* Besciamella

Beet greens
    leek soup with basil topping, 207
Beets
    Chioggia beet and radicchio salad, 93–94
    golden, risotto with pink radicchio and, 108–9
Besciamella
    herb, vegetable crespelle topped with, al forno,
      159–62
    herb-infused, sformato of young cauliflower and,
      165–66
Bitter orange gelato with mint leaves, 186–87
Black pepper, pasta with fava beans, parsley, butter,
    and, 215
Borage, 15, 188, 216
    artichokes, wild spring greens, and yellow potato
      stufato, 228
    crespelle filled with sautéed lettuces and ricotta
      topped with crisped prosciutto, 220–21
    rice, fava bean, and spring greens soup, 208–9
    risotto with borage leaves, carrot slivers, and
      pancetta, 216–17
Borlotti beans. *See also* Lamon beans
    assorted green chicory soup with pancetta and, 100
    fresh borlotti bean puree with sautéed Catalogna
      chicory, 226–27
Bread. *See also* Crostini; Panini
    bread "lasagna," 45–46
    crunchy bread topping, spaghettini with wild
      fennel, hot red pepper, and, 212–13
    mushrooms and bread slices on rosemary branch
      skewers, 55–56
    rosemary-scented rustic bread cubes, Lacinato kale
      soup with, 98–99
    zuppa della salute, 149
Bresaola involtini, 84
Broccoflower. *See* Broccoli; Cauliflower
Broccoli
    insalata di rinforzo, 95–96
    Romanesco, sformato of goat cheese and, 167–68
    Romanesco, spaghetti with black olives and, 101–2
Broccoli rabe, 171

cima di rapa with black olives and fresh bay leaves, 171

in lemon cream, 174

orecchiette with cima di rapa and hot red pepper, 103

panini with greens, black olives, and ricotta, 180–81

passato of cannellini beans and cima di rapa, 151

Broth, vegetable, with fennel, herbs, and dried Parmesan cheese rind, 97

Burrata with garnishes, 195

Candied whole kumquats, 126

panna cotta with, 130

Candy-sweet chopped fresh tomatoes, 65

Cannellini beans, passato of cima di rapa and, 151

Capers, 13, 66

Caprese salad

fall, 88

spring, 204

summer, 30–31

winter, 143

Caprino, ricotta and, layered with fresh basil leaves, 24–25

Carpaccio, zucchini, with almonds, 29

Carrots

red carrots sott'aceto with hot red peppers, 183; insalata di rinforzo with, 95–96

red carrots with honey and balsamic vinegar, 230

risotto with borage leaves, carrot slivers, and pancetta, 216–17

Catalogna chicory. *See also* Chicory

Pugliese, with red onion and salame, 177

sautéed, fresh borlotti bean puree with, 226–27

Cauliflower

insalata di rinforzo, 95–96

sformato of green cauliflower and goat cheese, 167–68

sformato of young cauliflower and herb-infused besciamella, 165–66

spaghetti with black olives and, 101–2

Caviar, warm avocados on the half-shell with, 200–201

Ceci. *See* Chickpeas

Celery

tubetti la favorita, 40

Cheese. *See also specific types*

burrata with garnishes, 195

ricotta and caprino layered with fresh basil leaves, 24–25

Cherry tomatoes, 12, 39

avocado on the half-shell, 34

barley soup with summer herbs, 36

little golden tomatoes sautéed with green and black olives and parsley, 53

orecchiette with little yellow tomatoes and parsley, 39

summer caprese salad, 30–31

sun-dried, 63

Chestnuts

red wine sciroppo, 184

Chickpeas

baked chickpeas in butter with rosemary sprigs, 172–73

ceci crisped in hot herbed extra virgin olive oil, 139

ditalini with tomatoes and, al forno, 156

Chicory. *See also* Endive; Escarole; Radicchio

artichokes, wild spring greens, and yellow potato stufato, 228

assorted green chicory soup with borlotti beans and pancetta, 100

autumn antipasto basket, 82

Catalogna, sautéed, fresh borlotti bean puree with, 226–27

crespelle filled with sautéed lettuces and ricotta topped with crisped prosciutto, 220–21

insalata di campo, 205

misticanza salad, 202

Pan di Zucchero salad, Giovanni's, 89–90

Pan di Zucchero salad with mint, orange zest, and hard-cooked egg, 114–15

Garlic
and bay leaves, young fennel with, 119
grilled wild mushrooms with winter savory and,
112
mustard greens all'aglio, 233
Gelato
bitter orange, with mint leaves, 186–87
Meyer lemon, topped with fresh figs and pistachios,
69–70
mint, topped with shavings of darkest chocolate,
71–72
Goat cheese
ricotta and caprino layered with fresh basil leaves,
24–25
sformato of green cauliflower and, 167–68
Golden raisins macerated in grappa, 127
Gorgonzola
warm crostini topped with Dolcelatte Gorgonzola
butter, 87
Granita, Meyer lemon, 73
Grapes
autumn antipasto basket, 82
Grappa
golden raisins macerated in, 127
grappa-soaked raisins, fettuccine with sautéed
radicchio, truffle oil, and, 105
Gratin, turnip (turnip tiella), 120
Green beans with European-style butter and basil
leaves, 52
Greens. See also specific types
artichokes, wild spring greens, and yellow potato
stufato, 228
crespelle filled with sautéed lettuces and ricotta
topped with crisped prosciutto, 220–21
mustard greens all'aglio, 233
panini with greens, black olives, and ricotta,
180–81
rice, fava bean, and spring greens soup, 208–9
Green tomatoes, 13, 106
pizza with red and green tomatoes, 123
risotto with, 106–7

Hazelnuts
winter caprese salad, 143
Herb flowers
frittata fiorita, 51
warm avocados on the half-shell, 200–201
Herbs, 14, 75. See also specific herbs
barley soup with summer herbs, 36
ceci crisped in hot herbed extra virgin olive oil, 139
garden herb pizza with Parma prosciutto topping,
60–61
herb and Parmesan custards with truffle oil,
163–64
herb besciamella, vegetable crespelle topped with, al
forno, 159–62
herb-infused besciamella, sformato of young
cauliflower and, 165–66
pasta with almost every herb in the garden, 41–42
pizza verde with artichoke hearts and herbs, 236
potato, olive, and ricotta torta, 47–48
spinach sautéed with spring herbs, 231
tiny herb frittatas, 22–23
vegetable broth with fennel, herbs, and dried
Parmesan cheese rind, 97
winter, fettuccine with wild mushrooms and,
152–53
Honey
Adriatic figs stuffed with stracchino cheese with, 81
red carrots with balsamic vinegar and, 230
Hot red pepper(s)
fresh peas with wild fennel and, 229
orecchiette with cima di rapa and, 103
red carrots sott'aceto with, 183
spaghettini with wild fennel, crunchy bread
topping, and, 212–13
whole braised young fennel with extra virgin olive
oil and, 234

Insalata di campo, 205
thin Parmesan frittata topped with, 224
Insalata di rinforzo, 95–96
Involtini, bresaola, 84

Orecchiette
  with cima di rapa and hot red pepper, 103
  with little yellow tomatoes and parsley, 39
Oregano, 75, 133, 189. *See also* Herbs
  bread "lasagna," 45–46
  ditalini with chickpeas and tomatoes al forno, 156
  ditalini with fresh peas, grated pecorino, and home-dried Italian oregano, 211
  green olive and Meyer lemon relish, 182
  home-dried, 64
  potato and escarole salad, 147
  summer caprese salad, 30–31

Pancetta
  assorted green chicory soup with borlotti beans and, 100
  risotto with borage leaves, carrot slivers, and, 216–17
Pan di Zucchero chicory, 89, 144. *See also* Chicory
  autumn antipasto basket, 82
  salad, Giovanni's, 89–90
  salad, with mint, orange zest, and hard-cooked egg, 144–45
Panini: fall, 124; spring, 237; summer, 62; winter, 180–81
  with greens, black olives, and ricotta, 180–81
  with grilled zucchini, ricotta salata, and basil, 62
  with Italian peppers and provolone, 124
  panino with mozzarella and parsley and almond relish, 237
Panna cotta with candied kumquats, 130
Parmesan
  herb and Parmesan custards with truffle oil, 163–64
  radicchio di Castelfranco with toasted almonds and warm butter, 91
  rind, vegetable broth with fennel, herbs, and, 97
  salad of radicchio leaves and nasturtiums with new-crop walnuts, 92
  thin Parmesan frittata topped with fresh field salad, 224

zucchini carpaccio with almonds and, 29
Parsley, 14, 134. *See also* Herbs
  and almond relish, 240; panino with, 237
  bread "lasagna," 45–46
  fresh fava beans with mint, marjoram, thyme, and, 232
  fresh ricotta with basil and, 19
  little golden tomatoes sautéed with green and black olives and, 53
  orecchiette with little yellow tomatoes and, 39
  parsley and rice salad, 32–33
  pasta with fava beans, butter, black pepper, and, 215
  pasta with young artichokes, white wine, and, 104
  pizza verde with artichoke hearts and herbs, 236
  risotto verde, 44
  rolled thin frittata filled with ricotta and, 49–50
  tubetti and Umbrian lentil soup, 150
Passato of cannellini beans and cima di rapa, 151
Pasta: fall, 101–5; spring, 211–15; summer, 37–42; winter, 152–56
  ditalini with chickpeas and tomatoes al forno, 156
  ditalini with fresh peas, grated pecorino, and home-dried Italian oregano, 211
  with fava beans, parsley, butter, and black pepper, 215
  fettuccine with sautéed radicchio, grappa-soaked raisins, and truffle oil, 105
  fettuccine with tomato and truffled anchovy butter, 154–55
  fettuccine with wild mushrooms and winter herbs, 152–53
  orecchiette with cima di rapa and hot red pepper, 103
  orecchiette with little yellow tomatoes and parsley, 39
  pasta tossed with ricotta and erbette, 214
  pasta with almost every herb in the garden, 41–42
  spaghettini with basil leaves and strands of lemon zest, 37

spaghettini with wild fennel, hot red pepper, and crunchy bread topping, 212–13

spaghetti with Romanesco broccoli and black olives, 101–2

spaghetti with tomato sauce and fresh basil leaves, 38

tubetti and Umbrian lentil soup, 150

tubetti la favorita, 40

with young artichokes, parsley, and white wine, 104

Pears

saffron pears poached in wine, 128

Peas, fresh

ditalini with grated pecorino, home-dried Italian oregano, and, 211

with wild fennel and hot red pepper, 229

Peppers, 32. *See also* Hot red pepper(s)

panini with Italian peppers and provolone, 124

"Pesto," dried fig and toasted almond, 125

Pine nuts

whole escarole stuffed with currants, sun-dried tomatoes, and, 175–76

Pino's pizza, 57–58

Pinzimonio, 196

Pistachios, Meyer lemon gelato topped with fresh figs and, 69–70

Pizza: fall, 123; spring, 235–36; summer, 57–61; winter, 178–79

dough for, 58–59

garden herb, with Parma prosciutto topping, 60–61

Pino's pizza, 57–58

pizza verde with artichoke hearts and herbs, 236

with potato and arugula, 178–79

with red and green tomatoes, 123

topped with fresh ricotta and arugula, 235

Plant lists

fall, 80

spring, 194

summer, 18

winter, 138

Portobello mushrooms

grilled, with winter savory and garlic, 112

mushrooms and bread slices on rosemary branch skewers, 55–56

Potato(es)

artichokes, wild spring greens, and yellow potato stufato, 228

and escarole salad, 147

pizza with arugula and, 178–79

potato, olive, and ricotta torta, 47–48

soup with new potatoes, saffron, basil, and mascarpone, 35

Preserves. *See* Condiments

Prosciutto

crisped, crespelle filled with sautéed lettuces and ricotta topped with, 220–21

garden herb pizza with Parma prosciutto topping, 60–61

La Baronessa's roses, 20–21

Provolone, panini with Italian peppers and, 124

Radicchio, 108, 121

autumn antipasto basket, 82

Chioggia beet and radicchio salad, 93–94

grilled, warm Lamon beans with, 169–70

pink, risotto with golden beets and, 108–9

radicchio di Castelfranco with toasted almonds and warm butter, 91

salad of radicchio leaves and nasturtiums with new-crop walnuts, 92

sautéed, fettuccine with grappa-soaked raisins, truffle oil, and, 105

warm crostini topped with Dolcelatte Gorgonzola butter, 87

whole Treviso radicchio in browned butter, 121

winter caprese salad, 143

Radishes, radish leaves, 195, 197

burrata with garnishes, 195

fresh-pulled radishes stuffed with green olive butter, 197–98

frittata with tender radish leaves, 222–23

Lamon bean salad, 146

spring caprese salad, 204